The Trump Revolt

Make America Great

Putting America First in a Woke World

James T. Wallace

Table of Contents

Introduction

The Trump Revolt Make America Great Again Putting America First in a Woke World examines the unprecedented clash between two powerful movements that have reshaped American culture, politics, and national identity: the populist surge of America First and the progressive wave of woke politics. This ideological divide has driven deep rifts within the country, touching nearly every aspect of American life—from policies on trade and immigration to discussions on social justice, equality, and inclusivity. In recent years, these movements have grown from niche ideologies into full-fledged cultural forces, with America First rallying behind nationalism, traditional values, and economic protectionism, while woke politics promotes social awareness, diversity, and systemic change.

At the heart of this conflict lies a question that has challenged America since its founding: What does it mean to be American? For some, it's about preserving the nation's historical identity, championing sovereignty, and defending the freedoms they believe have long defined the American experience. For others, it's about re-envisioning America as a more inclusive society that addresses past injustices and reflects the evolving demographics and values of its people. As each side pushes forward with its vision, the nation finds itself navigating one of the most polarized periods in modern history.

This book seeks to explore the roots of these opposing ideologies, their motivations, and the powerful cultural forces that sustain them. We'll delve into the rise of Donald Trump and the birth of the America First doctrine, examining the policies, rhetoric, and social dynamics that fueled his movement. Likewise, we'll analyze the growth of woke politics and the broader social justice movement, tracing its influence through institutions, corporations, and communities across the nation.

But this book goes beyond simply documenting the clash of ideologies; it aims to understand the complex dynamics that drive each side. What are the genuine fears, hopes, and grievances that fuel these movements? Why have traditional avenues of compromise and dialogue become so difficult to sustain? And perhaps most importantly, is there a way forward?

Through a balanced exploration of both perspectives, *The Trump Revolt: Putting America First in a Woke World* encourages readers to consider the implications of this cultural conflict. Whether you align with America First, woke politics, or find yourself somewhere in between, this book invites you to reflect on what these ideologies reveal about America's evolving identity and its potential future. This is not a call to choose sides; rather, it's a call to understand the forces at play, to acknowledge the complexity of modern American identity, and to recognize the essential challenge of building a nation that can accommodate—and even thrive on—its diversity.

As we embark on this journey, remember that America's strength has always been its capacity to confront change head-on. By engaging with these ideas and seeking to understand opposing viewpoints, we take the first step toward bridging divides and moving forward as a truly united nation.

Chapter 1: The Birth of the 'America First' Doctrine

Introduction to Trump's Political Rise and the Origins of the 'America First' Doctrine

The rise of Donald Trump as a political figure and eventual president of the United States was nothing short of a seismic shift in the American political landscape. Before his campaign for the presidency, Trump was best known as a real estate mogul, television personality, and celebrity, far removed from the traditional political class. His decision to run for president in 2016 was initially met with skepticism from political pundits, media outlets, and even within the Republican Party. However, Trump's message, particularly his emphasis on the "America First" doctrine, struck a chord with millions of voters who felt left behind by the status quo in Washington.

At its core, the "America First" doctrine is rooted in the concept of national sovereignty, economic protectionism, and prioritizing American interests above global obligations. Although Trump often framed this as a fresh, bold direction for U.S. policy, the idea of "America First" was not new. Its origins can be traced back to earlier periods of American history, particularly during the isolationist movements of the early 20th century, most notably in the lead-up to World War II.

In Trump's political rise, however, "America First" took on a more contemporary meaning, tailored to the anxieties and concerns of 21st-century Americans. The doctrine was a direct response to the perceived failures of globalization, multiculturalism, and interventionist foreign policies that dominated both Republican and Democratic administrations in recent decades. It tapped into the frustration of working-class Americans who felt that their economic prospects had been sacrificed on the altar of free trade agreements, unchecked immigration, and foreign military engagements.

The Political Landscape Before Trump

To understand Trump's rise and the emergence of the "America First" doctrine, it's essential to grasp the political and social dynamics in the United States leading up to the 2016 election. By the mid-2010s, the country was deeply divided, with a significant portion of the population feeling alienated from the political elite. Despite economic recovery following the 2008 financial crisis, income inequality was rising, and many working-class Americans—particularly in rural areas and industrial heartlands—felt that they had been left behind.

These frustrations were exacerbated by the rapid pace of demographic change, the increasing influence of progressive ideologies, and the growing sense that America's global role was costing more than it was delivering. Many Americans, particularly those outside urban centers, began to feel that their country was no longer recognizable—politically, culturally, and economically.

On the political front, the Republican Party had for years been grappling with its identity, caught between traditional conservative values and the demands of a rapidly changing electorate. The party had long championed free-market capitalism, interventionist foreign policies, and social conservatism, but these values were increasingly seen as disconnected from the reality faced by many of its base voters.

Trump's entry into the political arena was perfectly timed. His rhetoric did not align with traditional conservative orthodoxy, and that was precisely what gave him an edge. He distanced himself from establishment Republicans by embracing a more populist, nationalist message that resonated with the electorate's desire for change. This approach, centered on the notion of "America First," positioned Trump as an outsider, unafraid to challenge the political and media elites.

The Historical Roots of "America First"

While Trump modernized the "America First" doctrine to fit contemporary concerns, the roots of the philosophy stretch back nearly a century. The phrase "America First" gained prominence during the 1930s and early 1940s, as the United States grappled with its role on the global stage. At the time, many Americans were skeptical of becoming involved in World War II. The America First Committee, a prominent isolationist group, advocated for staying out of foreign entanglements, focusing instead on domestic issues.

This isolationist sentiment was fueled by the belief that America's involvement in World War I had been a mistake—a costly venture that ultimately did not serve the country's interests. Although the America First Committee disbanded after the attack on Pearl Harbor, the underlying ideas of prioritizing American interests and avoiding foreign intervention persisted in certain corners of American politics.

Fast-forward to the 21st century, and the same isolationist impulses found new relevance. Many Americans were weary of the wars in Iraq and Afghanistan, which were seen as quagmires with no clear end in sight. Meanwhile, free trade agreements like NAFTA were blamed for the decline of manufacturing jobs and the erosion of the middle class. These conditions created fertile ground for the revival of the "America First" philosophy—this time under the banner of Donald Trump.

Trump's Adaptation of "America First"

What set Trump apart from past advocates of "America First" was his ability to blend economic nationalism with cultural populism. In his 2016 campaign speeches, Trump frequently railed against globalism, which he framed as a system rigged against the American worker. He criticized multinational trade deals, which he claimed benefited foreign countries at the expense of American jobs. He promised to renegotiate or abandon deals that did not put American interests first.

Trump also tapped into growing concerns about immigration, both legal and illegal, which he argued threatened American workers and undermined national security. His promise to "build the wall" along the U.S.-Mexico border became a central and highly symbolic element of his campaign, reinforcing the idea that America needed to protect its borders and its people from external threats.

However, Trump's version of "America First" was not purely economic. It also encompassed a cultural dimension, as he positioned himself as a defender of traditional American values against the encroachment of progressive, "woke" ideologies. His attacks on political correctness, identity politics, and left-wing activism resonated with voters who felt that their cultural identity was under siege.

In this sense, Trump's "America First" was more than a policy doctrine—it was a rallying cry for millions of Americans who felt disenfranchised by the cultural, economic, and political shifts of the past few decades. By presenting himself as the champion of this movement, Trump was able to build a base of loyal supporters who were willing to overlook his unconventional style and focus on his message of national renewal.

The birth of the "America First" doctrine in the Trump era was both a response to and a rejection of the status quo in American politics. By channeling the frustrations of a disillusioned electorate, Trump tapped into a deep well of nationalist sentiment, reshaping the Republican Party and altering the trajectory of U.S. politics. His political rise and the adoption of "America First" would go on to define not only his presidency but also the broader ideological battles that continue to shape America today.

Historical Context: How American Nationalism and Populism Set the Stage for Trump's Movement

To fully understand the political phenomenon that became Donald Trump's "America First" doctrine, we must delve into the historical currents of American nationalism and populism. These intertwined ideologies have long played a pivotal role in shaping the country's political landscape, particularly during times of economic uncertainty and cultural shifts. Trump's ascendancy was not a sudden or isolated event but rather the culmination of decades, if not centuries, of nationalist and populist sentiments that periodically resurface in American politics.

The Roots of American Nationalism

Nationalism in the United States can be traced back to the country's founding. The American Revolution itself was an expression of nationalist ideals—an assertion of self-determination and the right of a distinct group of people to govern themselves, free from the control of an external empire. This idea of American exceptionalism, the belief that the United States has a unique and superior role to play on the world stage, has persisted throughout the nation's history.

In the 19th century, American nationalism found expression in the doctrine of Manifest Destiny, the belief that the United States was destined to expand across the North American continent. This expansion was seen not only as a fulfillment of the nation's potential but as a moral obligation to spread democracy and civilization. The Civil War, while a divisive and destructive conflict, was also a war over the very definition of the American nation. The eventual victory of the Union preserved the idea of a strong, centralized national identity, laying the groundwork for a more unified, though often contentious, nationalism in the years that followed.

By the early 20th century, American nationalism became more intertwined with the country's growing global influence. During World War I, President Woodrow Wilson promoted the idea of making the world "safe for democracy," signaling a shift toward a more interventionist nationalism. Yet, the aftermath of the war saw a retreat into isolationism, with many Americans questioning the wisdom of international entanglements. This tension between isolationist and interventionist strands of nationalism would continue to play out in U.S. politics, including during the Trump era.

The Populist Tradition in American Politics

Parallel to the growth of nationalism in the United States was the rise of populism—a political ideology that champions the interests of the "common people" against what is perceived as a corrupt and out-of-touch elite. Populism has historically emerged during periods of economic hardship or rapid societal change, when large swaths of the population feel alienated from those in power.

One of the earliest expressions of populism in American history was the populist movement of the late 19th century. This movement grew out of the struggles of farmers and laborers who felt marginalized by the industrial revolution and the rise of powerful corporate interests. The People's Party, often referred to as the Populist Party, advocated for policies such as government control of the railroads, a graduated income tax, and direct election of U.S. senators—ideas that would later be incorporated into the mainstream political system.

Although the Populist Party itself faded after the 1896 election, the populist ethos remained a potent force in American politics, reemerging during times of economic and social upheaval. The Great Depression, for instance, saw the rise of figures like Huey Long, who capitalized on populist anger toward the wealthy elite, proposing radical wealth redistribution plans under the slogan "Every Man a King."

In the post-World War II era, populism found new life in the political movements of the 1960s and 1970s, particularly among those who felt left behind by the civil rights movement, cultural liberalization, and economic globalization. George Wallace's 1968 presidential campaign, with its emphasis on law and order and its opposition to desegregation, drew heavily on populist themes, appealing to disaffected working-class white voters.

The Intersection of Nationalism and Populism in the Late 20th Century

The late 20th century saw the convergence of nationalist and populist ideas in ways that would set the stage for Trump's political movement. The post-Cold War period brought rapid globalization, economic restructuring, and demographic changes that fundamentally altered the American economy and society. While the U.S. remained the world's preeminent superpower, many Americans felt that the benefits of globalization were unevenly distributed, with the elite profiting at the expense of the middle and working classes.

The North American Free Trade Agreement (NAFTA), signed into law in 1993, became a lightning rod for this discontent. Critics argued that free trade deals like NAFTA encouraged the offshoring of American manufacturing jobs, leaving domestic workers, particularly in the industrial Midwest, vulnerable to economic displacement. This economic anxiety was compounded by increasing immigration, which some Americans saw as a threat to their cultural identity and economic security.

At the same time, the U.S. became embroiled in costly and prolonged military conflicts, most notably in Iraq and Afghanistan.

These wars, sold to the public on the basis of national security and spreading democracy, became deeply unpopular as the human and financial costs mounted. Many Americans began to question the wisdom of interventionist foreign policies and the idea that the U.S. should act as the world's policeman.

In this context, nationalist and populist sentiments began to reemerge with renewed vigor. Pat Buchanan, a conservative political commentator and three-time presidential candidate, was one of the early proponents of a modern "America First" platform. Buchanan's campaigns in the 1990s emphasized economic protectionism, immigration control, and non-interventionist foreign policies—many of the same themes that would later define Trump's platform. Though Buchanan never gained widespread political traction, his ideas laid the groundwork for what was to come.

The Obama Years and the Rise of the Tea Party

The presidency of Barack Obama, the nation's first African American president, marked a significant cultural and political shift in the U.S. While Obama was hailed by many as a symbol of progress, his presidency also sparked a backlash among certain segments of the population. The financial crisis of 2008 and the subsequent recession deepened economic inequalities, and while the economy recovered under Obama, many Americans felt that the benefits of the recovery were not reaching them.

The Tea Party movement, which emerged in the early years of Obama's presidency, was a populist response to what was perceived as government overreach, high taxation, and uncontrolled spending. Though ostensibly focused on economic issues, the Tea Party also tapped into broader cultural anxieties, including fears about immigration, globalization, and the changing demographic makeup of the country.

By the time Trump entered the political arena in 2015, these populist and nationalist currents had created a fertile environment for his message. The rhetoric of "draining the swamp," building a wall, and renegotiating trade deals resonated deeply with voters who felt disenfranchised by both the Democratic and Republican establishments. Trump's ability to blend economic populism with nationalist pride allowed him to tap into the anger and frustration that had been brewing for years.

The historical context of American nationalism and populism provided the foundation for Trump's political rise and the emergence of the "America First" doctrine. From the early days of the American Republic to the populist movements of the late 19th century, these ideologies have shaped the nation's political landscape, often surfacing during periods of economic and cultural upheaval. Trump's success in 2016 was not an anomaly but rather the latest expression of these deeply rooted currents, reconfigured for a modern era of globalization, immigration, and political discontent. The stage was set, and Trump's message of putting America first would go on to redefine the country's politics for years to come.

Key Elements of the 'America First' Policy – Economic Protectionism, Immigration Control, and Foreign Policy Shifts

The "America First" doctrine that became the cornerstone of Donald Trump's presidency can be understood through a few key elements: economic protectionism, immigration control, and a significant shift in foreign policy. These three pillars defined Trump's approach to governing and resonated strongly with his base, which felt alienated by decades of globalist policies that appeared to benefit multinational corporations and foreign powers at the expense of the American worker and national sovereignty. The following sections outline these core elements and explore how they reshaped the American political and economic landscape.

Economic Protectionism: Protecting American Jobs

At the heart of Trump's "America First" agenda was a commitment to economic protectionism. Unlike previous administrations that embraced the principles of globalization and free trade, Trump's policies prioritized American industries and workers by imposing tariffs, renegotiating trade deals, and encouraging companies to bring manufacturing jobs back to the United States.

One of the most notable actions in this regard was Trump's renegotiation of the North American Free Trade Agreement (NAFTA). Since its implementation in 1994, NAFTA had been widely criticized by segments of the American workforce, particularly in the manufacturing and agricultural sectors. Critics argued that the agreement led to the outsourcing of jobs to Mexico, where labor was cheaper, leaving American workers in vulnerable positions. Trump capitalized on these grievances, vowing to replace NAFTA with a more equitable deal that would benefit American workers.

In 2020, the Trump administration successfully implemented the United States-Mexico-Canada Agreement (USMCA), which sought to address many of the concerns raised by NAFTA's critics. The USMCA included provisions to increase wages for auto workers in Mexico, strengthen labor protections, and encourage more production of goods within the United States. The agreement was lauded by Trump's supporters as a major victory for American labor, while critics noted that the overall economic impact was relatively modest compared to the sweeping promises made during his campaign.

Another hallmark of Trump's economic protectionism was his use of tariffs as a tool to defend American industries. Trump frequently criticized China for engaging in unfair trade practices, accusing the country of manipulating its currency and stealing American intellectual property. In response, his administration imposed tariffs on billions of dollars' worth of Chinese goods. The goal was twofold: to protect American manufacturers from cheap Chinese imports and to pressure China into changing its trade practices.

While the tariffs led to a temporary boost for some American industries, such as steel and aluminum, they also had unintended consequences. American consumers and businesses that relied on imported goods saw prices rise, and retaliatory tariffs from China hurt U.S. farmers, particularly those in the soybean and pork industries. The trade war with China became one of the defining economic battles of Trump's presidency, embodying both the promise and the pitfalls of economic protectionism.

Trump's protectionist policies extended beyond tariffs and trade deals. He also championed tax cuts and deregulation as ways to incentivize domestic production and boost the economy. The Tax

Cuts and Jobs Act of 2017, which lowered the corporate tax rate from 35% to 21%, was intended to make the U.S. more competitive in the global market and encourage companies to reinvest in American infrastructure. While the tax cuts were praised by business leaders and many economists for stimulating short-term growth, they were also criticized for disproportionately benefiting the wealthy and contributing to the national deficit.

Immigration Control: Protecting Borders and National Identity

Perhaps the most contentious and visible element of Trump's "America First" policy was his focus on immigration control. From the earliest days of his campaign, Trump framed immigration as a central issue, both in terms of economic security and national identity. He argued that unchecked immigration, particularly from Latin America, was harming American workers by depressing wages and taking jobs that should go to U.S. citizens. Additionally, Trump emphasized the need to secure the country's borders to prevent crime, drug trafficking, and terrorism.

The most iconic symbol of Trump's immigration policy was the proposed construction of a border wall along the U.S.-Mexico border. Throughout his 2016 campaign, Trump repeatedly promised that the wall would be built and that Mexico would pay for it. While this promise was never fully realized, the Trump administration did manage to construct several hundred miles of new or replacement border barriers. The wall became a powerful political symbol, representing not just physical security but also a broader assertion of American sovereignty and control over who enters the country.

Beyond the wall, Trump implemented several executive orders aimed at curbing both legal and illegal immigration. One of the most controversial was the "Muslim Ban," a policy that restricted travel to the U.S. from several predominantly Muslim countries. While the administration framed the policy as a necessary measure for national security, critics condemned it as discriminatory and xenophobic. The policy faced numerous legal challenges but was ultimately upheld by the Supreme Court in 2018.

Trump's administration also pursued aggressive measures to crack down on illegal immigration. The "zero tolerance" policy at the southern border, which resulted in the separation of migrant children from their families, sparked widespread outrage and condemnation from human rights organizations. The policy was part of a broader effort to deter illegal immigration by making the consequences of crossing the border without authorization more severe.

In addition to these high-profile actions, Trump's administration sought to reduce legal immigration by cutting the number of refugees admitted to the U.S. and making it more difficult for immigrants to qualify for asylum. These measures were framed as necessary steps to protect American workers and resources, but they also fueled a heated national debate about the role of immigration in American society and the country's historical identity as a nation of immigrants.

Foreign Policy Shifts: Prioritizing National Sovereignty Over Globalism

The third pillar of the "America First" doctrine was a fundamental shift in U.S. foreign policy. Trump's approach to international relations was defined by his skepticism of multilateral organizations, international alliances, and global institutions that, in his view, diluted American sovereignty and forced the U.S. to bear an unfair burden of responsibility.

One of Trump's earliest foreign policy moves was to withdraw the United States from the Trans-Pacific Partnership (TPP), a major trade agreement negotiated by the Obama administration. Trump argued that the TPP would have been a disaster for American workers, outsourcing jobs to countries with cheaper labor costs. His withdrawal from the agreement signaled a clear break from the previous administration's globalist agenda and reinforced his commitment to bilateral trade deals that he believed would better serve American interests.

Trump's skepticism of international alliances was also evident in his approach to NATO. He repeatedly criticized the alliance for relying too heavily on U.S. military support while other member nations failed to meet their financial obligations. In public speeches, Trump called on NATO countries to contribute more to their own defense, warning that the U.S. would not continue to shoulder the bulk of the costs. This rhetoric was a significant departure from the more cooperative tone of previous U.S. presidents and raised concerns about the future of the alliance.

Perhaps the most significant foreign policy shift under Trump was his approach to international agreements on climate change. In 2017, Trump announced that the U.S. would withdraw from the Paris Climate Agreement, arguing that the deal placed an undue burden on American businesses and workers while allowing countries like China and India to continue polluting with fewer restrictions. This move was widely condemned by environmentalists and world leaders but was celebrated by Trump's supporters as a reaffirmation of national sovereignty and a rejection of globalism.

Trump's foreign policy, much like his domestic agenda, was guided by the belief that the United States had been taken advantage of on the world stage for too long. By withdrawing from international agreements, renegotiating trade deals, and demanding that allies pay more for their own defense, Trump sought to reassert American power and independence.

The key elements of Trump's "America First" policy—economic protectionism, immigration control, and foreign policy shifts—represented a dramatic departure from the norms of both Republican and Democratic administrations that preceded him. By prioritizing American workers, securing the country's borders, and reasserting national sovereignty, Trump built a movement that resonated with millions of Americans who felt left behind by globalization and the shifting cultural landscape. These policies, while controversial, were central to the "America First" doctrine and laid the foundation for the political battles that would define his presidency.

When Donald Trump first introduced his "America First" doctrine during his 2016 presidential campaign, it ignited intense and immediate reactions from both supporters and critics. These early responses set the stage for the cultural and political clashes that would dominate Trump's presidency and continue to shape the American political landscape long after he left office. The doctrine, rooted in nationalism, economic protectionism, and immigration control, touched on many of the raw nerves present in the country at the time, drawing fervent supporters and fierce detractors. Understanding these early reactions is crucial to grasping the forces that polarized the country and led to the deep ideological divides that defined the Trump era.

Supporters: A Call to Reclaim American Sovereignty

For many of Trump's supporters, the "America First" doctrine was a long-overdue recognition of the grievances that had been simmering for years. Trump's message resonated most strongly with working-class Americans, particularly in rural and industrial areas that had seen jobs disappear due to globalization, outsourcing, and the decline of manufacturing. His promises to bring jobs back to the U.S., renegotiate trade deals like NAFTA, and impose tariffs on countries like China were seen as tangible solutions to the economic anxieties these voters faced.

Trump's emphasis on immigration control, especially his controversial call to "build the wall" along the U.S.-Mexico border, was another key point of attraction for his supporters. Many believed that illegal immigration was not only taking jobs away from American citizens but also contributing to crime and the erosion of traditional American values. By focusing on immigration as a national security issue, Trump tapped into a sense of fear and frustration, particularly among those who felt that their communities were changing in ways they could no longer control.

In addition to economic and immigration concerns, Trump's supporters appreciated his unabashed nationalism and rejection of political correctness. His "drain the swamp" rhetoric, which promised to clean up corruption and remove the influence of career politicians, resonated with voters who felt alienated from both parties and disillusioned with the government. His status as a political outsider, combined with his blunt, combative style, was seen as a refreshing alternative to what many perceived as the overly cautious, polished politicians who dominated Washington, D.C.

For these supporters, the "America First" doctrine represented a reclamation of sovereignty—both in terms of national borders and economic independence. Trump was seen as the champion of the forgotten "real" Americans who had been left behind by a political system that catered to elites, globalists, and foreign interests. His promise to put American interests first was not just a policy stance but a rallying cry for a movement that aimed to reshape the very fabric of American society.

Critics: Fears of Isolationism, Racism, and Global Retrenchment

While Trump's "America First" message was greeted with enthusiasm by his base, it provoked an equally strong reaction from his critics. For many, the doctrine represented a dangerous retreat into isolationism, nativism, and xenophobia. Critics feared that Trump's rejection of international agreements, such as the Paris Climate Accord and the Trans-Pacific Partnership, would weaken America's global standing and undermine decades of diplomatic efforts that had helped maintain peace and stability.

The rhetoric around immigration, in particular, became a flashpoint for criticism. Trump's calls to build a border wall and implement travel bans on predominantly Muslim countries were seen as divisive and discriminatory. Human rights organizations, immigrant advocacy groups, and a significant portion of the Democratic Party condemned these policies as racist and xenophobic, warning that they would lead to the demonization of immigrants and foster an atmosphere of intolerance. The "zero tolerance" policy that resulted in the separation of migrant children from their families at the border became a symbol of what critics saw as the cruel and inhumane application of the "America First" doctrine.

On the economic front, many economists and trade experts warned that Trump's protectionist measures, particularly his tariffs on Chinese goods, would backfire, harming American consumers and businesses. Critics argued that the tariffs would lead to higher prices for everyday goods, disrupt global supply chains, and spark retaliatory actions from trading partners, potentially leading to a trade war. Some pointed out that while Trump's policies might protect certain industries in the short term, they would ultimately hurt the economy by reducing competition and innovation.

Critics also took issue with Trump's foreign policy approach, which they viewed as undermining America's role as a global leader. His disdain for multilateral organizations like NATO and his praise for authoritarian leaders like Russia's Vladimir Putin alarmed many in the foreign policy establishment. They feared that Trump's brand of nationalism would erode long-standing alliances, embolden adversaries, and make the world less stable. Trump's decision to withdraw from international agreements, such as the Iran nuclear deal, was seen as evidence that his "America First" approach would lead to greater instability in regions like the Middle East.

The Cultural Divide: The Rise of Woke Politics and Identity-Based Criticism

As Trump's "America First" doctrine became more prominent, it also sparked a significant cultural backlash, particularly among younger, more progressive Americans. The rise of what has been termed "woke" politics, focused on social justice, racial equity, and the recognition of systemic discrimination, was directly at odds with the themes of nationalism and traditionalism that underpinned Trump's message. For those who embraced the tenets of woke politics, Trump's emphasis on reclaiming American identity and sovereignty was seen as a coded call for the preservation of white, male-dominated power structures.

The cultural clash that ensued was not merely about policy differences—it was about competing visions of America's identity and future. On one side, Trump's supporters saw themselves as defending a version of America rooted in economic independence, national pride, and a shared cultural heritage. On the other side, Trump's critics viewed his policies as an attack on the progress made toward inclusion, diversity, and the dismantling of systemic inequalities.

This divide was often exacerbated by the media, with outlets that leaned left and right offering drastically different interpretations of Trump's actions and the consequences of his "America First" agenda. Conservative media outlets celebrated Trump's policies as bold, necessary, and effective, while liberal media framed them as dangerous, regressive, and often outright harmful. This polarization in media coverage contributed to a broader societal divide, where even basic facts and events were interpreted through highly partisan lenses.

Setting the Stage for Cultural and Political Clashes

The early reactions to Trump's "America First" doctrine laid the groundwork for the intense cultural and political clashes that would define his presidency. Supporters saw his policies as a necessary correction to decades of failed globalist policies, while critics viewed them as a dangerous step backward into isolationism, racism, and authoritarianism. These divergent perspectives fueled not only policy debates but also deeper conflicts about what it meant to be American and who had the right to define that identity.

As the cultural battles intensified, Trump's presidency became a symbol of the broader struggle between traditional American values and the progressive ideals of a rapidly changing society. The "America First" doctrine was both a political platform and a reflection of a growing populist movement that sought to reclaim national sovereignty in an increasingly globalized world. Meanwhile, the opposition to Trump's policies became emblematic of a broader push for social justice, inclusion, and a more interconnected global community.

The stage was set for a political and cultural war that would play out in every facet of American life—from policy debates in Washington to protests in the streets and battles for control of cultural narratives in the media. As Trump's presidency progressed, these early reactions solidified into deeply entrenched positions, making compromise and consensus seem increasingly out of reach.

The early reactions to Trump's "America First" doctrine were as polarized as the country itself, with supporters seeing it as a necessary corrective to globalization and progressive policies, while critics viewed it as a regressive and dangerous ideology. These initial responses laid the foundation for the cultural and political clashes that would come to define Trump's presidency, as competing visions of America's future collided in the national consciousness. The "America First" doctrine, far from being a mere policy platform, became the centerpiece of a larger ideological battle over the soul of the nation.

Chapters 2 The Rise of Woke Culture

Definition and Historical Evolution of Woke Culture and Its Principles, such as Social Justice, Diversity, and Inclusivity

The concept of "woke culture" has become a prominent and polarizing element in modern American society. Although often associated with contemporary movements for social justice, diversity, and inclusivity, the roots of woke culture can be traced back through decades, even centuries, of struggle for equality and fairness. To understand the significance of woke culture in today's social and political climate, we must first define what it entails, explore its historical evolution, and examine the core principles that drive it.

Defining Woke Culture

At its most basic level, "woke" is a term derived from African American Vernacular English (AAVE), originally meaning to be awake or alert to social injustice and systemic inequalities. Over time, it evolved to signify an awareness of the various forms of oppression that impact marginalized groups, including issues related to race, gender, sexuality, and economic class. Woke culture, then, represents the collective attitudes, beliefs, and actions taken by individuals and groups who actively work to recognize and address these injustices.

Woke culture is grounded in the idea that society is layered with structures of power that disproportionately benefit certain groups—often white, male, heterosexual, and affluent individuals—while marginalizing others. Those who identify as "woke" are committed to challenging these structures, whether through activism, policy advocacy, or cultural shifts, to create a more equitable society. Central to woke culture are the principles of social justice, diversity, and inclusivity, which shape its approach to reforming or dismantling systems perceived as unjust.

Historical Evolution of Woke Culture

The evolution of woke culture is deeply rooted in the history of social justice movements in the United States, each of which contributed to a growing awareness of inequality and the need for societal change.

Early Civil Rights Movements

Woke culture's origins can be traced back to early abolitionist movements in the 19th century. Abolitionists were among the first to challenge the existing social and economic systems that normalized slavery and racial subjugation. Their efforts set the foundation for later movements by establishing the moral argument against institutionalized inequality. Following the Civil War and the abolition of slavery, African American leaders and activists continued to advocate for civil rights, pushing back against segregation, voter suppression, and racial violence.

The Civil Rights Movement of the 1950s and 1960s marked a significant milestone in the evolution of woke culture. Leaders such as Martin Luther King Jr., Rosa Parks, and Malcolm X highlighted the structural barriers that Black Americans faced and called for systemic change. Their work not only focused on legal equality but also on the broader goal of dismantling societal structures that enabled discrimination. This era introduced the concept of intersectionality—the understanding that various forms of discrimination (racial, economic, gender-based) intersect and amplify inequality.

Women's Liberation and Feminism

The feminist movement, particularly the second wave in the 1960s and 1970s, was instrumental in shaping the principles of woke culture. While the first wave of feminism in the early 20th century focused on basic rights, such as suffrage, the second wave addressed deeper issues related to gender roles, workplace equality, reproductive rights, and sexual freedom. Feminists argued that patriarchy, or male-dominated power structures, was a root cause of gender-based discrimination and that achieving equality required addressing these entrenched societal norms.

Feminism also expanded the idea of inclusivity, emphasizing that equality could not be achieved if women from marginalized groups—such as women of color or those from lower socioeconomic backgrounds—were left behind. This emphasis on inclusivity within feminism laid the groundwork for later movements that stressed the importance of considering all forms of diversity when addressing social issues.

LGBTQ+ Rights Movement

The LGBTQ+ rights movement, which gained momentum after the Stonewall Riots in 1969, contributed significantly to the development of woke culture. LGBTQ+ activists fought against discrimination in housing, employment, healthcare, and public accommodations. Their advocacy highlighted the systemic barriers that LGBTQ+ individuals faced and challenged societal norms around gender and sexuality.

Over time, the movement evolved to include a broader understanding of gender and sexual diversity, advocating for the rights of transgender and non-binary individuals. This expansion of LGBTQ+ rights brought attention to the concept of inclusivity in ways that reshaped societal norms and values, making it clear that an equitable society must respect and accommodate a variety of gender identities and sexual orientations.

Economic and Labor Rights

Woke culture is also informed by labor movements that sought economic justice and workers' rights. The labor rights movement in the early 20th century fought for fair wages, safe working conditions, and reasonable hours, which were seen as basic human rights. Organizations such as the American Federation of Labor (AFL) and the Industrial Workers of the World (IWW) advocated for the rights of working-class Americans who were often exploited by corporate power and unregulated capitalism.

In recent years, this emphasis on economic justice has been revived by movements such as Occupy Wall Street, which called attention to income inequality and corporate greed. The slogan "We are the 99%" became a rallying cry for economic reform and highlighted the vast disparities between the wealthiest Americans and the rest of the population. This economic dimension of woke culture is crucial, as it underscores that social justice also includes the pursuit of financial and class equity.

Contemporary Social Justice Movements

In the 21st century, woke culture has been heavily influenced by movements such as Black Lives Matter (BLM), which emerged in response to police violence and systemic racism. BLM amplified the conversation about racial injustice, advocating for policy reforms and social change. This movement, and others like it, has used social media to galvanize support, educate the public, and pressure policymakers.

The #MeToo movement also played a key role, bringing awareness to issues of sexual harassment and assault, particularly in workplaces. The movement highlighted how gender inequality and power imbalances contribute to systemic abuse. It pushed organizations and institutions to adopt stricter policies and accountability measures to protect women and marginalized communities from exploitation.

Core Principles of Woke Culture: Social Justice, Diversity, and Inclusivity

Today, woke culture is guided by a few core principles, each of which shapes the actions and goals of those who identify with the movement.

Social Justice

At the heart of woke culture is a commitment to social justice, which seeks to address and rectify systemic inequalities. Social justice involves creating equitable opportunities for marginalized groups, removing barriers to access, and challenging laws and policies that perpetuate discrimination. Woke culture's commitment to social justice is visible in calls for criminal justice reform, educational equity, healthcare access, and economic fairness. Activists advocate for policies that correct historical injustices, such as reparations for descendants of enslaved people, as well as protections for vulnerable communities.

Diversity

Diversity, a key tenet of woke culture, stresses the importance of including individuals from a variety of backgrounds, including different races, genders, sexual orientations, cultures, and abilities. Woke culture emphasizes that diverse perspectives enrich society and create more innovative and responsive institutions. In practice, this principle drives efforts to increase representation in media, politics, workplaces, and educational institutions, with the goal of making these spaces reflective of society's varied demographics.

Inclusivity

While diversity emphasizes representation, inclusivity goes further, focusing on creating environments where all people feel valued and respected. Inclusivity addresses the power dynamics that may prevent marginalized individuals from fully participating in society. This principle promotes the idea that an equitable society does not just tolerate differences but actively embraces them. Inclusivity efforts are often seen in initiatives to make workplaces, schools, and public spaces accessible and welcoming to all, regardless of race, gender, ability, or identity.

The principles of woke culture—social justice, diversity, and inclusivity—are rooted in a long history of struggles for equality and fairness. Woke culture builds on these movements, broadening the focus to address the interconnected forms of discrimination that exist today. Its rise reflects an evolving societal awareness that systemic inequities affect a wide array of communities and that achieving a just society requires conscious, collective action. As woke culture continues to influence social and political discourse, it remains a powerful, though contentious, force in shaping the values and priorities of contemporary America.

Key Events and Movements That Fueled the Rise of Woke Culture, Including Black Lives Matter, Me Too, and the Push for Environmental Justice

The rise of woke culture in the United States has been fueled by a series of transformative social movements and events that have drawn attention to various forms of injustice and inequality. Each of these movements highlights different aspects of social justice—racial, gender-based, environmental, and beyond—while collectively driving a broader cultural shift toward heightened awareness and advocacy for systemic change. Among the most influential of these movements are Black Lives Matter, the #MeToo movement, and the push for environmental justice. Each of these movements has played a pivotal role in shaping the principles and goals of modern woke culture, emphasizing the need for structural change across multiple facets of society.

Black Lives Matter: Confronting Racial Injustice

One of the most powerful and globally recognized social justice movements of recent years, Black Lives Matter (BLM) emerged in 2013 as a response to the acquittal of George Zimmerman, the man who shot and killed Trayvon Martin, an unarmed Black teenager. The hashtag #BlackLivesMatter, created by activists Alicia Garza, Patrisse Cullors, and Opal Tometi, quickly gained traction on social media, sparking a nationwide conversation about racial injustice, police brutality, and the systemic discrimination faced by Black Americans.

The movement gained further momentum following a series of high-profile incidents in which Black individuals, such as Michael Brown, Eric Garner, and Freddie Gray, lost their lives during interactions with law enforcement. These cases brought national and international attention to the issues of police violence and institutional racism, galvanizing communities to demand accountability, transparency, and reform within the justice system.

In 2020, the tragic death of George Floyd, who died under the knee of a Minneapolis police officer, reignited the movement with unprecedented intensity. Protests erupted across the United States and around the world, with millions calling for justice and the end of systemic racism. This wave of activism led to widespread support for BLM, with many corporations, celebrities, and political leaders publicly endorsing the movement's goals. These protests brought conversations about racial justice into the mainstream, pressuring institutions to address discriminatory practices and promote racial equity within their organizations.

The influence of Black Lives Matter on woke culture is significant. It emphasized that societal structures—including policing, education, and housing—often perpetuate racial inequalities. The movement inspired a new generation of activists and brought racial justice to the forefront of American discourse, making it a core component of woke culture. The widespread calls for structural change, such as defunding or reforming police departments and addressing systemic bias, have encouraged both local and national leaders to consider policies aimed at achieving racial equality.

#MeToo: Addressing Gender Inequality and Sexual Misconduct

The #MeToo movement is another defining force in the rise of woke culture, shedding light on gender inequality and the pervasive issue of sexual harassment and assault. Although activist Tarana Burke originally coined the phrase "Me Too" in 2006 to support survivors of sexual violence, the movement gained global prominence in 2017 after numerous high-profile women in Hollywood spoke out about sexual abuse at the hands of influential producer Harvey Weinstein.

When actress Alyssa Milano encouraged survivors to share their experiences on social media using the hashtag #MeToo, it quickly went viral, revealing the widespread nature of sexual harassment and abuse across multiple industries. Thousands of women and men came forward with stories of workplace harassment, abuse, and misconduct, exposing patterns of behavior that had long been hidden or normalized.

The #MeToo movement's impact extended beyond Hollywood, prompting similar reckonings in politics, sports, media, and corporate sectors. Major companies began implementing stricter policies to prevent sexual harassment, and many public figures and corporate leaders were held accountable for their actions. The movement also inspired legislative changes, such as extending the statute of limitations for reporting sexual assault and implementing mandatory training on harassment prevention in the workplace.

#MeToo shifted societal norms, making it less acceptable to dismiss or ignore claims of harassment and abuse. It also helped dismantle a culture of silence and stigma around survivors, empowering individuals to speak out against wrongdoing without fear of retaliation. In the context of woke culture, #MeToo represents the commitment to gender equality and accountability, calling for a transformation in how society treats and supports survivors of sexual violence. It also emphasizes the need for systemic reform to address power imbalances that contribute to abuse and discrimination.

The Push for Environmental Justice: Linking Social and Ecological Health

While social justice movements often focus on issues like race, gender, and class, the push for environmental justice highlights the intersection between social inequity and ecological concerns. Environmental justice advocates argue that marginalized communities—particularly low-income and minority groups—are disproportionately affected by environmental hazards, including pollution, toxic waste, and the impacts of climate change.

The roots of environmental justice activism can be traced back to the 1980s, when residents of Warren County, North Carolina, protested the placement of a hazardous waste landfill in their predominantly Black community. This event is often cited as the beginning of the environmental justice movement, as it highlighted how marginalized communities are frequently targeted for environmentally harmful projects due to their lack of political power and resources.

The movement gained national attention in recent years due to issues like the Flint water crisis in Michigan, where residents—primarily low-income and Black—were exposed to lead-contaminated water due to government negligence. The crisis not only highlighted the environmental risks that disproportionately affect marginalized communities but also underscored the failure of authorities to protect these populations. Similarly, the rise of climate change activism has drawn attention to the fact that communities already vulnerable due to economic or racial factors are often the first and worst affected by natural disasters, extreme weather, and other climate impacts.

Today, environmental justice is a key component of woke culture, as it emphasizes the need for equitable access to clean air, water, and land. Environmental justice advocates call for policies that address pollution, climate change, and environmental degradation while prioritizing the needs of those most impacted. This push for environmental equity is visible in campaigns for green energy, reduced carbon emissions, and sustainable development that consider the needs of vulnerable communities. The movement underscores the principle that true social justice must encompass not only human rights but also the right to a safe, healthy environment.

Collective Impact on Woke Culture

Each of these movements—Black Lives Matter, #MeToo, and environmental justice—addresses a different facet of social justice, yet they are united by a common goal: to challenge and dismantle systems of inequality and oppression. Together, they have fueled the rise of woke culture, expanding its scope to include a wide range of issues that affect people on both individual and societal levels.

Black Lives Matter has brought racial justice and police reform to the center of woke culture, emphasizing the need for systemic change to address historical and ongoing discrimination. #MeToo has reinforced the importance of accountability, gender equality, and the fight against harassment and abuse, making it clear that social justice requires safe, respectful environments for all individuals. The environmental justice movement has broadened the concept of social equity by highlighting the environmental factors that contribute to inequality, advocating for policies that prioritize vulnerable communities and sustainable practices.

Woke culture, as shaped by these movements, reflects a multifaceted approach to social change. It encourages individuals and institutions to be vigilant in recognizing injustices across various spheres and to actively work toward a more inclusive, equitable society. This cultural shift has led to an increased focus on diversity, inclusion, and accountability, influencing everything from corporate policies to public discourse. While woke culture has its critics, its roots in these movements underscore a profound shift in societal values toward greater awareness, empathy, and action for systemic change.

The rise of woke culture is inseparable from the impact of transformative social movements like Black Lives Matter, #MeToo, and environmental justice advocacy. Each of these movements has brought essential issues to the forefront of public consciousness, challenging existing power structures and redefining social norms. Together, they illustrate the broad scope of woke culture, which seeks to address and resolve inequalities across race, gender, and environmental health. By recognizing these injustices and advocating for systemic reform, woke culture continues to shape a new vision for a more equitable society.

The Role of Social Media and Mainstream Media in Amplifying Woke Narratives and Shaping Public Discourse

In today's digital age, social media and mainstream media are powerful forces in shaping public discourse, particularly around socially charged issues like those central to woke culture. Through these platforms, narratives around social justice, diversity, inclusivity, and activism are not only amplified but also woven into the everyday consciousness of the public. Social media, with its ability to reach billions in real-time, and mainstream media, with its established authority and influence, work together to magnify the impact of woke culture, reinforcing its visibility and embedding its values into modern dialogue. This symbiotic relationship has enabled woke culture to grow from a grassroots movement into a global cultural phenomenon, sparking conversations, controversies, and shifts in policy and perception.

Social Media: The Megaphone of Modern Activism

Social media platforms such as Twitter, Instagram, Facebook, and TikTok have played a critical role in the rise of woke culture by providing a decentralized and accessible space for individuals to share ideas, mobilize support, and hold powerful institutions accountable. Unlike traditional media, social media operates in real time, allowing information to spread rapidly and enabling users to engage directly with content creators and other followers. This immediacy has transformed the way social movements operate, making it possible for a single hashtag or viral post to launch a movement.

Hashtag Activism

Hashtags like #BlackLivesMatter, #MeToo, #ClimateJustice, and #SayHerName have become synonymous with woke culture, serving as digital rallying cries that bring attention to specific issues. Hashtag activism allows users to amplify their voices by uniting under a common banner, making it easy for people around the world to find, share, and participate in discussions. A single post with a hashtag can attract millions of impressions, turning local issues into global conversations. For example, #BlackLivesMatter began as a small, grassroots movement but gained worldwide recognition through social media, becoming one of the most visible symbols of modern woke culture.

Viral Content and Storytelling

Social media's visual nature, especially on platforms like Instagram and TikTok, allows for powerful storytelling through images and videos. Videos of protests, testimonies from marginalized individuals, and eye-opening infographics are highly shareable and accessible, making it easy for users to engage with and understand complex issues. Viral content often compels viewers to confront uncomfortable truths, fostering empathy and awareness. For instance, videos documenting police brutality or environmental destruction can bring abstract concepts like systemic racism or climate justice into sharp focus, creating a visceral connection that inspires action.

Direct Mobilization and Fundraising

Social media is also a powerful tool for direct action, enabling users to quickly organize protests, raise funds, and create petitions. Platforms like Twitter and Facebook allow activists to coordinate events, share updates, and connect with like-minded individuals without relying on traditional organizational structures. This decentralized approach allows movements to grow organically, with individuals feeling empowered to contribute in their own ways. Fundraising efforts on platforms like GoFundMe have enabled activists and organizations to raise millions of dollars for causes like bail funds, legal aid, and community support, often within hours of going viral.

Influencer and Celebrity Amplification

Social media influencers and celebrities play a major role in amplifying woke narratives, as their massive followings give them the power to shape public opinion. When high-profile figures endorse social justice causes or participate in campaigns, their messages reach audiences that might not otherwise engage with these topics. Celebrities like Beyoncé, Lady Gaga, and Colin Kaepernick have used their platforms to champion woke culture causes, helping to normalize these discussions and drive wider acceptance of progressive values.

Through these mechanisms, social media has democratized woke culture, making it accessible to anyone with an internet connection. This accessibility has allowed traditionally marginalized voices to challenge dominant narratives, creating a space where individuals can freely express their views on social justice, advocate for reform, and participate in a global conversation.

Mainstream Media: The Authority of Public Discourse

While social media provides a decentralized platform for individual voices, mainstream media serves as the authoritative voice of public discourse, lending credibility and visibility to woke culture narratives. Television networks, newspapers, and online news outlets play a crucial role in framing issues, contextualizing movements, and shaping how the public perceives social justice initiatives.

Agenda-Setting and Framing

Mainstream media has the power to set the public agenda, deciding which issues receive coverage and how they are presented. By covering events like protests, legislative changes, and celebrity endorsements, mainstream media helps bring woke issues to the attention of a broader audience. The framing of these issues—whether as moral imperatives, political debates, or cultural shifts—greatly influences public perception. For example, the coverage of the #MeToo movement as a reckoning against systemic abuse in Hollywood not only informed the public but also sparked similar reckonings in other industries, from politics to tech.

Investigative Journalism and In-Depth Reporting

Mainstream media's capacity for in-depth reporting and investigative journalism provides a level of rigor and credibility that social media alone cannot. Detailed reports on issues like racial disparities in policing, environmental degradation in marginalized communities, or corruption in government policies offer well-researched perspectives that bolster woke culture narratives. Investigative journalism has the power to uncover hidden injustices, as was seen in the #MeToo movement, where media outlets like The New York Times and The New Yorker published exposés that brought years of abuse into public view. This type of reporting adds substance and weight to the issues raised on social media, providing readers with the facts necessary to make informed decisions.

Broadcasting Protests and Amplifying Movements

During major events, such as the George Floyd protests, mainstream media coverage brings real-time visibility to social justice movements, often reaching audiences who do not actively engage on social media. News outlets that cover protests, marches, and rallies provide legitimacy to these events, treating them as national or even international news. For instance, the widespread coverage of Black Lives Matter protests in 2020 demonstrated the movement's scale and significance, reinforcing its relevance and prompting governments, corporations, and individuals to take notice.

Expert Analysis and Opinion

Mainstream media often features expert opinions and analysis from academics, activists, and political figures, offering insights that enhance the public's understanding of woke issues. Talk shows, opinion columns, and interview segments allow for diverse perspectives on complex issues, from systemic racism to climate change. This type of coverage not only informs the public but also deepens the discourse, making it more difficult for individuals to ignore or dismiss woke culture narratives.

While mainstream media has traditionally been more cautious in its approach, the pressure to stay relevant in an age of social media has driven many outlets to adopt a more vocal stance on social justice issues. As such, mainstream media and social media now operate in a feedback loop: social media highlights issues that may not receive immediate coverage, and when mainstream media picks them up, it lends additional authority and reach to the narratives.

The Synergy of Social Media and Mainstream Media

The relationship between social media and mainstream media is synergistic, with each platform reinforcing and amplifying the other's impact on woke culture. Social media acts as a grassroots force, allowing individuals to raise awareness and drive action, while mainstream media provides the gravitas that elevates these issues into the public consciousness.

For example, during the #MeToo movement, many survivors initially shared their experiences on social media, creating a groundswell of voices that attracted media attention. Once mainstream outlets covered these stories, they sparked a wave of accountability that reached the highest levels of government, entertainment, and corporate sectors. Similarly, environmental justice issues often gain traction on social media before being picked up by news outlets, as was the case with the Dakota Access Pipeline protests. Once mainstream media highlighted the movement, it gained wider recognition and support.

This synergy has made woke culture an unavoidable part of contemporary society, influencing public opinion, corporate policies, and even government action. Social media provides the immediacy and inclusivity that engages the masses, while mainstream media provides the structure and legitimacy that make these issues part of the national agenda.

The rise of woke culture owes much to the amplification power of social media and mainstream media, which together shape public discourse and drive awareness of social justice issues. Social media enables grassroots mobilization and creates a space for marginalized voices, while mainstream media lends authority and structure to these conversations, making them accessible and credible to a wider audience. Through their combined influence, these platforms have transformed woke culture from a fringe ideology into a major force in modern society, impacting everything from personal beliefs to institutional policies. As both social and mainstream media continue to evolve, their role in amplifying woke narratives will undoubtedly shape the future of public discourse, ensuring that issues of justice, diversity, and inclusivity remain at the forefront of societal change.

Early Signs of Tension Between Woke Culture and Traditional American Values Espoused by the 'America First' Movement

As woke culture gained momentum in the United States, it began to clash with traditional American values associated with the 'America First' movement. This friction wasn't merely about differences in political opinions or social policy but rather a profound disagreement over the nation's identity, values, and direction. On one side, the America First movement emphasized national sovereignty, economic protectionism, and a return to conservative ideals. On the other, woke culture championed social justice, inclusivity, and systemic change, often questioning the foundations on which American society was built. These opposing visions of America set the stage for a culture war that would shape public discourse, policies, and the fabric of American society.

The Clash Over National Identity

One of the earliest and most visible points of contention between the America First movement and woke culture revolved around the concept of national identity. The America First movement, driven by populist and nationalist ideals, argued for a return to a traditional vision of America, grounded in patriotism, self-reliance, and cultural cohesion. Supporters believed that American greatness lay in its founding principles and that preserving these values was essential to maintaining national unity and strength.

In contrast, woke culture viewed the traditional narrative of American identity as outdated, exclusionary, and, in some cases, rooted in systemic injustice. Woke advocates argued that the historical narrative of America often glossed over its darker chapters, including slavery, colonialism, and racial discrimination. For many within woke culture, embracing a more diverse and inclusive America meant reexamining—and often challenging—

the traditional symbols, monuments, and historical accounts that had long represented the nation's identity.

The movement to remove or reinterpret historical monuments, such as statues of Confederate leaders, became a flashpoint in this cultural divide. For the America First supporters, these monuments represented an important part of the nation's history and heritage. Removing them, they argued, was an attempt to erase history and undermine traditional American values. Woke advocates, however, saw these monuments as glorifications of oppression and argued that taking them down was a step toward acknowledging and redressing the injustices that marginalized communities had suffered.

Diverging Views on Social Justice and Personal Responsibility

Another core area of tension between woke culture and the America First movement is the question of social justice versus personal responsibility. Woke culture emphasizes systemic inequality, pointing to structures that disproportionately benefit certain groups over others. This perspective advocates for policies and reforms aimed at addressing institutional barriers in areas like education, healthcare, employment, and criminal justice. Woke advocates argue that real equality requires proactive efforts to dismantle these barriers and create an environment where marginalized communities have equal opportunities.

The America First movement, on the other hand, generally favors a worldview rooted in individual responsibility and meritocracy. Supporters believe that America is a land of opportunity, where success is achievable through hard work and determination. From this perspective, government interventions aimed at correcting inequalities are often seen as overreach that fosters dependency rather than empowerment. America First advocates argue that prioritizing individual responsibility strengthens the nation by encouraging self-sufficiency and resilience, viewing government policies aimed at addressing systemic inequalities as counterproductive.

This divide is particularly evident in debates over affirmative action, welfare programs, and criminal justice reform. Woke culture advocates for policies that they believe would level the playing field for disadvantaged communities, while America First supporters see these policies as forms of reverse discrimination or government intrusion. The contrasting beliefs about fairness, responsibility, and the role of government create a fundamental ideological rift that has influenced policies and political discourse across the nation.

Patriotism and the Question of American Exceptionalism

Patriotism and the concept of American exceptionalism are also contentious points between the America First movement and woke culture. The America First philosophy holds that America is a unique nation with a distinct role in the world—a place of freedom, democracy, and opportunity that should remain true to its founding principles. Supporters of America First believe that promoting these values domestically and globally is vital for the nation's success and stability.

In contrast, woke culture takes a more critical approach to American exceptionalism. While not inherently unpatriotic, woke advocates argue that true patriotism includes acknowledging and addressing the country's flaws. For those aligned with woke culture, America's legacy includes both its achievements and its failures, and real progress requires confronting historical injustices to build a fairer and more inclusive society. This approach often includes questioning the narratives of American exceptionalism, as well as the impact of U.S. policies on marginalized communities, both domestically and internationally.

For example, events like the Vietnam War, the Iraq War, and various interventions in Latin America are often viewed by woke advocates as examples of American imperialism rather than exceptionalism. America First supporters, however, see these interventions as evidence of America's commitment to defending freedom and democracy around the world. This divergence over the meaning of patriotism and exceptionalism underscores a broader ideological divide about America's role on the global stage and what it means to be a patriot.

The Tension Between Traditional and Progressive Values

The cultural clash between America First and woke culture is also evident in the differing views on traditional versus progressive values. The America First movement often advocates for a return to traditional values, emphasizing family, religion, and a sense of moral clarity. Many of its supporters view these values as fundamental to maintaining social cohesion and national strength, arguing that progressive ideals, including woke culture, undermine the moral fabric of society.

Woke culture, however, is largely progressive in nature, championing values such as inclusivity, gender equality, LGBTQ+ rights, and multiculturalism. Woke advocates argue that traditional values often uphold outdated and exclusionary norms that do not reflect the diversity of modern society. They believe that progress means redefining societal norms to be more inclusive and that values must evolve to meet the needs of an increasingly diverse population.

This tension is particularly evident in debates over issues like same-sex marriage, transgender rights, and gender roles. America First supporters often argue that these issues challenge traditional values that have served as the foundation of American society.

Woke advocates, meanwhile, see these issues as fundamental rights, viewing the expansion of these rights as a reflection of America's commitment to freedom and equality for all. This ideological divide has become a battleground in cultural, legal, and political arenas, with each side seeking to assert its vision of what American values should be.

Free Speech and the Battle Over Cancel Culture

The concept of "cancel culture" has further deepened the rift between woke culture and the America First movement, creating a debate over free speech and accountability. Cancel culture refers to the practice of calling out and boycotting individuals, companies, or public figures who express views that are considered offensive or harmful. For proponents of woke culture, canceling is seen as a means of holding people and institutions accountable for promoting ideas or behaviors that perpetuate harm or discrimination.

America First supporters, however, argue that cancel culture undermines free speech and silences dissenting voices. They view it as an authoritarian tactic used to enforce ideological conformity and suppress viewpoints that do not align with progressive values. From this perspective, cancel culture is seen as antithetical to American ideals of freedom of expression, open debate, and the right to disagree.

High-profile cases, such as controversies surrounding comedians, academics, and business leaders, highlight the deep division over cancel culture. America First advocates argue that individuals should have the right to express unpopular or politically incorrect opinions without fear of professional or personal ruin, while woke advocates believe that harmful rhetoric must be confronted and discouraged to protect vulnerable communities. This battle over free speech has intensified in recent years, creating a contentious atmosphere in media, education, and entertainment.

The early signs of tension between woke culture and the America First movement reveal a deep ideological divide that goes beyond policy differences. These two perspectives represent fundamentally different visions of what America is and should become. While America First emphasizes tradition, national pride, and individual responsibility, woke culture advocates for inclusivity, social justice, and a reexamination of America's historical narrative. As these opposing viewpoints gained traction, they set the stage for a cultural and political clash that would influence public opinion, policies, and American identity. This battle continues to shape the discourse, highlighting the challenge of finding common ground in a society increasingly divided over its most basic values and ideals.

Chapter 3: Clash of Ideologies: Trump vs. The Woke Movement

Examination of the Ideological Clashes Between Trump's America First Policies and the Principles of Woke Culture

The ideological clash between Trump's America First policies and the principles of woke culture highlights two divergent visions for America's future. These opposing worldviews touch upon nearly every facet of society, from national identity to economic policy, social justice, and America's role on the global stage. The America First doctrine, with its emphasis on nationalism, traditional values, and economic protectionism, contrasts sharply with woke culture's focus on inclusivity, social justice, and systemic reform. This section examines the core ideological differences that fuel the conflict between these movements, revealing a deep divide in American society that goes beyond simple political disagreements.

Nationalism vs. Globalism

At the heart of the America First doctrine lies a strong sense of nationalism, advocating for a return to American self-reliance and a reduced involvement in global affairs. Trump's policies focused on protecting American interests, often at the expense of global alliances and multilateral agreements. For Trump and his supporters, prioritizing the United States meant strengthening its economy, safeguarding its borders, and reducing dependence on foreign nations. This perspective reflects a belief that American sovereignty and identity are paramount, and that globalization has compromised the well-being of the American people, particularly those in the working class.

Woke culture, on the other hand, tends to embrace a more global perspective, viewing interconnectedness as essential to addressing modern issues like climate change, human rights, and economic inequality. Woke advocates argue that America has a moral responsibility to support global causes and engage in multilateral agreements to promote equality and environmental sustainability worldwide. To them, nationalism is seen as a barrier to progress, one that ignores the realities of a globalized world where problems cross borders and require collective solutions.

This clash between nationalism and globalism reveals a fundamental divide in how each side views America's role in the world. For America First advocates, globalism represents a loss of control and a dilution of American identity. For woke culture supporters, globalism is essential for creating a more just and sustainable world. This ideological divide shapes debates on issues ranging from immigration and trade to climate agreements and foreign aid.

Traditionalism vs. Progressivism

Another core ideological conflict between America First and woke culture lies in their respective views on tradition and progress. America First is rooted in traditionalism, emphasizing the preservation of long-standing American values, such as individualism, family, faith, and patriotism. Trump's rhetoric often called for a return to a perceived "better" past, where these values were celebrated and the nation was unified under a shared cultural identity. Supporters of America First argue that upholding traditional values provides social stability, fosters a strong work ethic, and preserves what they see as the essence of the American spirit.

Woke culture, in contrast, champions progressive values, viewing change as necessary to create a more inclusive society. Woke advocates argue that traditional values often uphold outdated and oppressive norms that marginalize minority groups. From this perspective, progress means questioning and reforming these norms to reflect a more diverse, multicultural society. Issues such as LGBTQ+ rights, racial equity, gender equality, and religious inclusivity are central to the woke agenda, as advocates seek to build a society where all individuals have equal rights and opportunities.

This conflict over values is particularly evident in debates over cultural symbols, educational curricula, and social norms. For America First supporters, woke efforts to challenge traditional values are seen as a rejection of American heritage and an erosion of moral standards. Conversely, woke advocates view traditionalist stances as barriers to justice and equality, perpetuating inequality by holding on to exclusionary practices. This ideological clash has significant implications, shaping not only cultural norms but also laws and policies that affect everyday life in America.

Meritocracy vs. Systemic Change

The America First movement often espouses a meritocratic worldview, holding that success is achieved through hard work, talent, and personal responsibility. Trump's policies on issues like welfare reform, immigration, and affirmative action reflect this belief in self-sufficiency, with a focus on individual effort as the path to prosperity. For America First advocates, government interventions aimed at redistributing resources or addressing historical inequalities are seen as undermining meritocracy and creating dependency. They argue that providing too much government support fosters a culture of entitlement, rather than one of resilience and self-reliance.

Woke culture, however, challenges the notion of meritocracy, pointing to systemic inequalities that hinder marginalized communities from having equal opportunities. Woke advocates argue that factors like race, gender, and socioeconomic background create barriers that merit alone cannot overcome.

From this perspective, policies addressing systemic inequality—such as affirmative action, increased social welfare programs, and education reform—are essential for leveling the playing field. Woke culture views these interventions as necessary steps to dismantle the structural disadvantages that disproportionately affect certain groups, creating a society where success is genuinely accessible to all.

The debate between meritocracy and systemic change is evident in discussions on economic policies, educational access, and criminal justice reform. America First proponents tend to favor policies that reward individual effort and view systemic interventions as overreach. Woke culture advocates, however, see systemic reform as essential for building an equitable society. This clash shapes public policy and divides Americans on the best way to address issues like poverty, education disparities, and social mobility.

Patriotism vs. Accountability

The concept of patriotism is another area where America First and woke culture diverge significantly. America First supporters view patriotism as a duty to honor and protect the nation's legacy, celebrate its achievements, and preserve its heritage. Trump's speeches often appealed to a sense of national pride, calling on Americans to "make America great again" and to prioritize the country's interests. For many America First advocates, patriotism is an unqualified loyalty to the country, its history, and its symbols, which they see as embodying the American spirit.

Woke culture, however, promotes a different kind of patriotism—one that includes holding the country accountable for its shortcomings. Woke advocates argue that true patriotism involves recognizing and addressing historical injustices, such as slavery, racial discrimination, and gender inequality. This form of patriotism is rooted in a desire to improve the nation by acknowledging its flaws and striving to build a more just society. From this perspective, criticism is not an attack on America but rather an expression of hope and commitment to making the country better.

This clash between loyalty and accountability is evident in debates over issues like historical monuments, the national anthem, and the teaching of American history in schools. For America First supporters, efforts to critique or revise aspects of American history are seen as unpatriotic and an attempt to undermine national pride. For woke advocates, these efforts represent a necessary reckoning with the past to ensure a more inclusive future. The differing views on patriotism reveal a deep ideological divide over what it means to love and support one's country.

Free Speech vs. Safe Spaces

The debate over free speech versus safe spaces highlights the differing priorities of America First and woke culture. America First supporters emphasize free speech as a cornerstone of American democracy, arguing that all viewpoints should be expressed without fear of censorship or retribution. Trump's defense of free speech often resonated with those who felt that conservative viewpoints were being suppressed by a liberal-leaning media and academia. America First advocates argue that free speech is essential for robust debate and that efforts to restrict certain viewpoints, even offensive ones, undermine fundamental American freedoms.

Woke culture, however, places a strong emphasis on creating safe spaces that protect marginalized groups from hate speech, discrimination, and harm. Woke advocates argue that free speech should not be a license for speech that perpetuates harm or marginalization, especially toward vulnerable communities. They believe that certain forms of speech, such as racist or sexist language, can create hostile environments and perpetuate inequality. For woke culture, protecting marginalized individuals from harm often takes precedence over absolute free speech, leading to policies and practices that restrict harmful language in schools, workplaces, and online platforms.

This clash over free speech and safe spaces plays out in universities, social media platforms, and public discourse, creating a complex debate over the boundaries of expression. America First supporters view restrictions on speech as a form of censorship, while woke advocates see them as necessary protections for marginalized voices. This ideological divide illustrates the competing priorities of each movement: one prioritizes freedom of expression, while the other emphasizes creating inclusive and respectful environments.

The ideological clashes between Trump's America First policies and the principles of woke culture reveal two fundamentally different visions for America. While America First advocates prioritize nationalism, traditional values, meritocracy, patriotism, and free speech, woke culture emphasizes globalism, progressivism, systemic reform, accountability, and protection for marginalized groups. These opposing ideologies touch on nearly every aspect of American life, from individual rights and responsibilities to national identity and America's role on the world stage.

As these competing worldviews continue to shape public discourse, they reflect a broader cultural and political divide within the United States. The clash between America First and woke culture is not merely a policy debate; it is a battle over the soul of the nation, its values, and its future. Each side believes its vision represents the path to a better America, making this ideological conflict one of the most defining and consequential of our time.

Case Studies of Specific Policy Areas: Immigration (the Border Wall, Travel Bans), Economic Nationalism (Trade Wars, Tariffs), and Social Issues (LGBTQ Rights, Gender Policies)

The clash between Trump's America First policies and the principles of woke culture is perhaps most evident in specific policy areas where each side's priorities, values, and approaches stand in direct opposition. In key areas like immigration, economic nationalism, and social issues, the ideological divides come into sharp focus, creating a battleground over what America should represent and how it should function. These case studies of immigration, economic nationalism, and social issues illustrate the broader conflict between Trump's vision for America and the progressive values espoused by woke culture.

Immigration: The Border Wall and Travel Bans

Immigration policy became a defining feature of the Trump administration and a focal point for the clash with woke culture. Trump's approach to immigration, particularly his proposals for a border wall and travel bans, reflected the America First emphasis on national sovereignty, security, and a desire to control who enters the country. These policies were met with strong resistance from woke advocates, who saw them as exclusionary, discriminatory, and contrary to the values of inclusivity and compassion for marginalized groups.

The Border Wall

One of Trump's most iconic and polarizing campaign promises was to build a wall along the U.S.-Mexico border, a symbol of his commitment to securing America's borders and preventing illegal immigration. For Trump and his supporters, the border wall represented more than a physical barrier; it was a declaration of American sovereignty and a stand against what they saw as uncontrolled immigration that threatened American jobs, culture, and security. The wall was portrayed as a way to protect American citizens from crime, drug trafficking, and economic competition from undocumented workers.

Woke culture advocates, however, viewed the border wall as a deeply divisive and xenophobic measure. For them, the wall symbolized exclusion, intolerance, and an attempt to criminalize individuals seeking a better life in the United States. Many argued that the wall disregarded the complexities of immigration, including the push factors that drive people to leave their home countries. Additionally, critics claimed that the wall ignored America's identity as a nation of immigrants and dismissed the humanitarian obligation to provide asylum to those fleeing violence and persecution. The clash over the border wall thus epitomized the ideological divide between a nationalistic approach to immigration and a perspective rooted in inclusivity and empathy.

Travel Bans

Another contentious policy that highlighted the ideological clash was Trump's executive order restricting travel from several predominantly Muslim-majority countries, known as the "Muslim Ban." Initially framed as a measure to protect national security, the travel ban barred entry to the U.S. from certain countries believed to pose a risk of terrorism. For Trump and his supporters, the ban was seen as a necessary step in protecting American lives and preventing the entry of individuals who might pose a threat to national security.

From the perspective of woke culture, however, the travel ban was discriminatory and unfairly targeted Muslim communities. Critics argued that the ban fueled Islamophobia, reinforcing harmful stereotypes and creating unnecessary barriers for individuals from affected countries. Woke advocates also pointed out that the ban contradicted America's values of religious freedom and nondiscrimination, as it disproportionately impacted people based on their nationality and faith. The travel ban became a rallying point for civil rights groups and progressive advocates who viewed it as a violation of constitutional rights and an expression of prejudice under the guise of national security.

Economic Nationalism: Trade Wars and Tariffs

Economic nationalism formed another cornerstone of Trump's America First agenda, with trade wars and tariffs as key tools to protect American industries and reduce dependence on foreign imports. Trump's administration sought to reshape the global economic order by renegotiating trade deals, imposing tariffs on imports, and encouraging domestic production. This approach contrasted sharply with the principles of woke culture, which emphasize global cooperation, fair labor practices, and environmental sustainability in trade policies.

Trade Wars

Trump's trade war with China was one of the most significant expressions of economic nationalism in his administration. Frustrated with what he saw as unfair trade practices, including intellectual property theft and currency manipulation, Trump imposed tariffs on hundreds of billions of dollars' worth of Chinese goods. The goal was to reduce the U.S. trade deficit with China, protect American manufacturing, and encourage companies to bring production back to the United States.

While Trump's supporters saw the trade war as a bold move to prioritize American jobs and industry, woke advocates viewed it as short-sighted and potentially harmful to both American consumers and global economic stability. Many progressive economists argued that the tariffs led to higher prices for American consumers and retaliatory tariffs that hurt American farmers and exporters. Additionally, woke culture proponents criticized the trade war for focusing solely on economic competition without addressing labor rights or environmental concerns. From their perspective, a more ethical approach to trade would involve collaborative efforts to improve labor conditions, reduce environmental impact, and promote sustainable growth—principles that the America First approach largely ignored.

Tariffs on Allies

Trump's imposition of tariffs on imports from traditional allies, such as the European Union, Canada, and Mexico, further exemplified his economic nationalism. These tariffs, particularly on steel and aluminum, were justified by the administration as necessary to protect national security and safeguard American industries. However, they sparked tensions with allied nations and raised questions about the future of U.S. relationships with its traditional partners.

Woke culture advocates criticized these tariffs as economically and diplomatically damaging. Many argued that targeting allies undermined the spirit of international cooperation and risked alienating partners who shared America's commitment to democratic values. From a woke perspective, economic policies should prioritize global solidarity and collaboration over unilateral actions that could strain international relations. The tariffs highlighted the divide between Trump's America First policies, which emphasized American economic self-interest, and the globalist values of woke culture, which call for mutually beneficial partnerships and shared responsibility.

Social Issues: LGBTQ Rights and Gender Policies

Social issues, including LGBTQ rights and gender policies, are another area where the clash between Trump's policies and woke culture principles is starkly visible. Trump's administration took a conservative approach to these issues, often rolling back protections for LGBTQ individuals and emphasizing traditional gender norms. These actions were perceived by many woke advocates as direct attacks on progress made toward inclusivity and equality, further fueling the ideological divide.

LGBTQ Rights

The Trump administration's stance on LGBTQ rights was marked by a series of controversial policies, including the decision to ban transgender individuals from serving in the military. This policy was justified by the administration as necessary to maintain military readiness and reduce costs, and it was praised by social conservatives who viewed it as a return to traditional military standards.

Woke culture advocates, however, saw the ban as a discriminatory policy that undermined the rights and dignity of transgender individuals. LGBTQ rights groups argued that the ban sent a message of exclusion, reinforcing harmful stereotypes and stigmatizing transgender Americans. The ban became a rallying point for woke advocates, who pushed for policies that recognize and protect the rights of all individuals, regardless of gender identity. This clash over LGBTQ rights highlighted the broader ideological divide: while America First policies emphasized tradition and perceived practicality, woke culture prioritized inclusivity and equal rights as fundamental to a just society.

Gender Policies and Title IX

The Trump administration also introduced changes to Title IX guidelines related to how schools handle allegations of sexual misconduct, implementing policies that increased protections for those accused of harassment and assault. These changes, according to the administration, were intended to ensure due process and prevent unfair punishment for the accused.

Woke culture advocates criticized these Title IX revisions, arguing that they made it more difficult for victims of harassment and assault to come forward and seek justice. From their perspective, the changes undermined protections for survivors, sending a discouraging message to victims. Advocates for gender equality argued that policies should be structured to empower and support survivors, rather than focusing primarily on the rights of the accused. This clash over Title IX policies illustrated the fundamental divide between America First's emphasis on traditional notions of fairness and woke culture's focus on supporting vulnerable groups and creating safe, supportive environments.

The case studies of immigration, economic nationalism, and social issues reveal the deep ideological conflict between Trump's America First policies and the principles of woke culture. Each policy area underscores the differing priorities and values of the two movements. America First policies, with their emphasis on national security, economic self-interest, and traditional values, stand in stark contrast to the inclusivity, global cooperation, and systemic reform that characterize woke culture.

These policy clashes are more than isolated disagreements; they reflect a broader struggle over the direction of American society. The opposing stances on immigration, economic policy, and social issues illustrate the challenges of bridging this divide, as each side pursues a vision for the nation that feels incompatible with the other. As these ideological battles continue to play out, they shape the future of American policy, culture, and identity, marking a profound turning point in the country's history.

How These Ideological Battles Played Out in the Media, with an Analysis of the Narratives from Both Pro-Trump and Woke Perspectives

The media has been a powerful battleground for the ideological clash between Trump's America First policies and the values of woke culture. Through cable news, social media, online publications, and print media, this battle has been fought on multiple fronts, shaping public opinion, amplifying narratives, and deepening divides. Both pro-Trump and woke perspectives have found platforms that reflect and reinforce their worldviews, creating echo chambers that further polarize the American public. Analyzing these narratives from both perspectives reveals the ways in which the media has both reflected and fueled this ideological conflict.

The Pro-Trump Media Narrative: Defending Nationalism, Tradition, and Sovereignty

Pro-Trump media outlets and personalities have framed the ideological battles around America First as a fight to preserve traditional American values against a perceived cultural takeover by woke culture. For these outlets, Trump's policies were portrayed as necessary correctives to what they saw as years of liberal overreach, globalization, and a progressive agenda that threatened the nation's identity and stability.

Immigration and Border Security

In pro-Trump media, immigration was often depicted as a critical issue of national security and sovereignty. Outlets like Fox News and Breitbart frequently emphasized the dangers of illegal immigration, framing the border wall and travel bans as essential tools to protect American citizens from crime, drug trafficking, and economic harm. The border wall was portrayed as a symbol of American strength and resolve, with Trump's commitment to its construction celebrated as a promise kept to his supporters.

In this narrative, woke opposition to immigration restrictions was portrayed as naïve, reckless, or even traitorous. Woke advocates were frequently described as undermining the rule of law and disregarding the safety and interests of American citizens in favor of globalist ideals. This framing sought to rally support for the America First agenda by appealing to patriotic sentiments, portraying immigration restrictions as essential to preserving American culture and protecting jobs.

Economic Nationalism and Trade Wars

Pro-Trump media outlets defended Trump's economic nationalism, including tariffs and trade wars, as necessary measures to protect American workers and industries. Outlets like The Daily Caller and conservative radio hosts like Rush Limbaugh and Sean Hannity argued that previous trade deals had sold out American interests, benefitting foreign nations and multinational corporations at the expense of the American middle class. Trump's renegotiation of trade deals and his tariffs on China were framed as long-overdue actions to restore American economic independence.

Woke culture's critique of these policies, which often focused on the global repercussions of tariffs and the potential economic harm to American consumers, was dismissed in pro-Trump media as elitist and out of touch. Supporters of America First policies argued that woke culture's emphasis on globalism and environmental concerns ignored the struggles of American workers who had been left behind by decades of deindustrialization. Pro-Trump media framed economic nationalism as a moral imperative, with Trump positioned as a champion of the "forgotten man" against a global elite.

Social Issues and Cultural Preservation

Social issues, including gender and LGBTQ rights, were often framed in pro-Trump media as part of a broader cultural war. Conservative outlets portrayed Trump's policies, such as the transgender military ban and the rollback of certain protections, as a defense of traditional values and the integrity of American institutions. The rise of woke culture, with its emphasis on inclusivity and progressive gender policies, was depicted as an attempt to undermine the nation's moral fabric.

In this narrative, woke culture was seen as a force that threatened to impose "political correctness" on American society, stifling free speech and eroding traditional values. Pro-Trump commentators often argued that woke culture was imposing an authoritarian agenda, where dissenting views on social issues were punished or silenced. By framing woke culture as a threat to individual liberties, pro-Trump media aimed to position America First policies as a stand for freedom against an oppressive, left-wing ideology.

The Woke Media Narrative: Advocating for Social Justice, Inclusivity, and Systemic Change

In contrast, media outlets that aligned with woke culture framed the ideological clash as a struggle for social justice, inclusivity, and systemic reform. For these outlets, Trump's America First policies represented a regressive force that sought to undo progress on civil rights, diversity, and environmental responsibility. Outlets like MSNBC, The New York Times, and online publications like Vox and HuffPost framed the America First agenda as a threat to marginalized communities and an obstacle to social progress.

Immigration and Human Rights

Woke-aligned media depicted Trump's immigration policies, including the border wall and travel bans, as cruel, discriminatory, and rooted in xenophobia. The media focused on human interest stories of immigrants and asylum seekers, highlighting the hardships faced by families separated at the border or refugees unable to enter the United States due to travel bans. This framing emphasized the human cost of Trump's policies, appealing to viewers' empathy and reinforcing the woke narrative of inclusivity and compassion.

In this context, the border wall was portrayed not as a symbol of American sovereignty but as a barrier to human rights and humanitarian values. Woke media argued that America's strength lay in its diversity and its legacy as a nation of immigrants, casting Trump's restrictive immigration policies as contrary to the nation's founding ideals. The coverage often included voices from immigrant advocacy groups, human rights organizations, and community activists who argued for more compassionate policies.

Economic Nationalism and Global Responsibility

Woke-aligned media criticized Trump's economic nationalism, particularly the trade wars and tariffs, as shortsighted and harmful to both Americans and global economic stability. Outlets like The Washington Post and NPR focused on the potential consequences of tariffs, such as higher prices for American consumers and retaliatory tariffs that hurt American farmers. Woke media argued that the America First approach ignored the interconnected nature of the global economy and failed to address broader issues like fair labor practices, environmental impact, and economic equity.

This framing positioned woke culture as the more ethical approach, advocating for trade policies that balanced American interests with global responsibilities. Woke media emphasized the need for economic policies that promote sustainable development, fair wages, and responsible production, often citing experts and economists who warned that isolationist policies could ultimately backfire. This narrative sought to portray Trump's economic nationalism as a reckless and isolationist approach that ignored the complexities of modern economics.

Social Issues and Civil Rights

Woke media's framing of social issues, particularly LGBTQ rights and gender policies, cast Trump's policies as a rollback of civil rights and a threat to marginalized groups. Trump's decisions, such as the transgender military ban and the administration's stance on gender identity, were depicted as discriminatory policies that endangered the rights and well-being of LGBTQ Americans. Publications like The Guardian, BuzzFeed News, and CNN emphasized the impact of these policies on vulnerable communities, portraying woke culture's push for inclusivity as essential to upholding American values of equality and justice.

In this narrative, Trump's America First policies on social issues were seen as part of a broader backlash against the progress made by civil rights movements. Woke media emphasized the importance of inclusivity, portraying any attempt to restrict LGBTQ rights or limit protections for gender diversity as a step backward. This framing positioned woke culture as the defender of equality, committed to creating a society that embraced and protected all identities, contrasting sharply with the traditionalist values promoted by America First.

The Media as an Echo Chamber: Reinforcing Divides

One of the most significant consequences of the media's role in these ideological battles is the creation of echo chambers, where audiences are exposed primarily to narratives that align with their existing beliefs. Pro-Trump media reinforced the America First perspective by framing Trump's policies as a defense of American values and sovereignty against the threat of a radical, left-wing ideology. Woke-aligned media, on the other hand, portrayed Trump's policies as regressive and dangerous, positioning woke culture as the ethical counterweight advocating for progress and inclusivity.

This polarization in media coverage deepened divides, with audiences increasingly consuming content that reinforced their worldview while dismissing opposing perspectives. Cable news networks like Fox News and MSNBC, social media platforms like Twitter, and online forums all contributed to this fragmentation, creating a media landscape where Americans are increasingly siloed into ideological camps.

The role of social media in particular has amplified these divides, as algorithms on platforms like Facebook and Twitter prioritize content that aligns with users' interests, leading them toward more extreme and reinforcing viewpoints. Hashtags, viral posts, and influential figures from both sides further intensified the clash, with each side framing the other as an existential threat to the future of the country.

The media has played an essential role in shaping and amplifying the ideological clash between Trump's America First policies and woke culture. Through their respective narratives, pro-Trump and woke-aligned media outlets have reinforced opposing perspectives on key issues like immigration, economic nationalism, and social issues, contributing to a polarized public. Each side sees itself as defending fundamental values—whether it's America First's emphasis on sovereignty, traditionalism, and self-reliance or woke culture's commitment to inclusivity, social justice, and systemic reform.

As these narratives continue to shape public discourse, they also deepen the cultural and political divides within American society.

The role of the media in this ideological battle underscores the difficulty of finding common ground in a society where information is increasingly filtered through partisan lenses. This clash in the media is not merely a reflection of ideological differences; it actively shapes them, creating an environment where understanding and compromise seem increasingly elusive.

The ideological clash between Trump's America First movement and woke culture has not only transformed political discourse but also deeply affected public perception, amplifying divisions within American society. As these two powerful and opposing worldviews gained prominence, they fueled a cultural battle that left little room for neutrality, forcing Americans to align themselves with one side or the other on issues ranging from national identity to social justice. This polarization has reshaped American society, contributing to strained relationships, fractured communities, and an increasingly segmented media landscape. This section explores how the clash between these ideologies has affected public perception, dividing Americans along political, cultural, and social lines and intensifying polarization across the nation.

The Polarization of Identity and Values

One of the most profound effects of the ideological clash between America First and woke culture has been the polarization of identity and values in the United States. This polarization has redefined how many Americans perceive themselves and others, with individuals increasingly associating their identity with political or cultural beliefs. For example, to be "pro-America First" often connotes a set of values that emphasize nationalism, traditionalism, and economic self-reliance. Conversely, identifying with woke culture is associated with progressive values, such as social justice, inclusivity, and global responsibility.

This ideological polarization has transformed the very concept of American identity, creating a divide between those who view America as a land defined by traditional values and self-determination and those who see it as a nation that must acknowledge its flaws and work toward a more inclusive, equitable future. As a result, Americans have become increasingly divided on fundamental questions of national purpose, patriotism, and historical interpretation. This divide has made it more difficult for individuals to find common ground, as they are not only debating policies but also the core principles and values that define their identities.

The Role of the Media in Shaping Perceptions

Media coverage has played a critical role in shaping public perceptions of the America First-woke culture divide. By framing issues through partisan lenses, media outlets have encouraged viewers to adopt polarized viewpoints, reinforcing existing biases and deepening ideological divides. Conservative media outlets, such as Fox News, often present America First values as a defense against the "radical left" and woke ideologies, portraying these as existential threats to American traditions, freedom of speech, and patriotism. Progressive media outlets, such as MSNBC, tend to frame Trump's America First movement as a regression into isolationism, xenophobia, and discrimination, positioning woke culture as the morally superior alternative.

The media's role in amplifying these perspectives has led to echo chambers where individuals consume information that aligns with their beliefs and dismiss opposing viewpoints as biased or manipulative. This selective exposure to information has created a cycle of reinforcement, where public perception becomes more rigid, and individuals increasingly define themselves and others based on their alignment with either America First or woke values. This dynamic has contributed to a sense of ideological entrenchment, where even moderate positions are rare and compromise feels impossible.

Social Media and the Rise of Cancel Culture

Social media has intensified polarization by creating platforms where public opinion can be amplified, scrutinized, and challenged in real time. Platforms like Twitter, Facebook, and Instagram have become arenas for ideological warfare, where the America First and woke culture factions clash openly and publicly. The rapid spread of information, often in the form of short, emotionally charged posts, has fostered an environment of immediacy and intensity, encouraging individuals to respond quickly and passionately rather than thoughtfully.

Cancel culture has become a notable feature in this environment, where individuals and public figures can face backlash, boycotts, or "cancellation" for expressing views that are seen as incompatible with woke ideals. Supporters of America First argue that cancel culture is a form of censorship that silences conservative voices and discourages open debate. Woke advocates, however, see cancel culture as a tool for holding individuals and institutions accountable for harmful or regressive views. The presence of cancel culture on social media has made the clash between America First and woke ideologies even more personal, as individuals are increasingly judged not only for their actions but also for their beliefs and affiliations. This has contributed to a climate of fear and caution, where people feel compelled to hide or suppress views that could provoke backlash, further entrenching divisions and reducing opportunities for open dialogue.

Political Polarization and Partisan Loyalty

The clash between America First and woke culture has also led to heightened political polarization, with individuals showing increased loyalty to their chosen political party and hostility toward the opposition. For many Americans, political affiliation has become synonymous with identity, values, and social group, creating an "us vs. them" mentality that discourages compromise and collaboration. The ideological divide has reinforced party loyalty to an extent that it shapes opinions on nearly every issue, from immigration and trade to healthcare and climate change.

Public perception has shifted to view the opposing political party not simply as a group with different ideas but as an existential threat to the future of the nation. For America First supporters, the Democratic Party is seen as the political arm of woke culture, a force that seeks to undermine American sovereignty, values, and stability. Conversely, those aligned with woke culture often view the Republican Party as a bastion of America First ideals that resist social progress and uphold outdated norms. This deep partisan divide has made it increasingly difficult for politicians to reach bipartisan agreements, as crossing party lines is often viewed as a betrayal of core values.

Fractured Communities and Family Strain

One of the more personal consequences of this ideological clash has been the impact on relationships within families, friendships, and communities. The polarization of America First and woke culture has permeated everyday interactions, leading to tensions and conflicts that strain bonds between individuals with differing viewpoints. Friends and family members who once enjoyed amicable relationships now find themselves divided by these powerful ideologies, with disagreements that go beyond policy and touch on deeply held beliefs about justice, morality, and the future of the nation.

For many, discussing politics or social issues has become a source of stress, often avoided altogether to prevent arguments. In some cases, ideological differences have led to the severing of relationships, as individuals feel that they can no longer relate to or understand friends or family members with opposing views. Communities that once shared common goals or values now find themselves fractured along ideological lines, with residents gravitating toward groups and networks that reinforce their beliefs. This segmentation has reduced opportunities for mutual understanding, increasing the sense of division and isolation felt by individuals on both sides of the America First-woke culture divide.

Increased Distrust in Institutions

The clash between America First and woke culture has also led to a growing distrust in American institutions, with each side questioning the integrity of entities they believe are aligned against their values. For America First supporters, institutions such as the media, academia, and even government agencies are often viewed as biased toward progressive or woke agendas, undermining conservative values and promoting an anti-American sentiment. This distrust has fueled skepticism toward sources of information and expertise that are perceived as "elitist" or unpatriotic.

Conversely, woke culture advocates view institutions like the criminal justice system, corporate America, and certain political structures as bastions of systemic oppression and inequality. They argue that these institutions perpetuate historical injustices and that reform or even dismantling of these structures is necessary to create a more just society. This skepticism has led to calls for systemic reform in nearly every area of public life, from policing to corporate governance, with the goal of addressing what they see as entrenched discrimination.

This widespread distrust in institutions has had far-reaching consequences, contributing to a breakdown in social cohesion and a loss of shared beliefs about the reliability of public systems. As trust in institutions declines, Americans have increasingly turned to alternative sources of information and community, further fragmenting society and reinforcing polarized viewpoints.

The Normalization of Conflict and the Decline of Civil Discourse

The clash between America First and woke culture has also normalized conflict in American society, making polarization and ideological division seem like permanent fixtures. Civil discourse has become a casualty of this ideological battle, as debates over issues often devolve into personal attacks, assumptions, and stereotyping. In the current climate, disagreement is less about differing viewpoints and more about questioning the character or motives of those with opposing beliefs. This decline in civil discourse has affected public discussions, social media interactions, and even formal debates, where personal attacks and dismissive language have become commonplace.

The acceptance of conflict as the "new normal" has made it more difficult for Americans to find common ground or engage in productive dialogue. Instead of fostering understanding or compromise, interactions between individuals with opposing views are often seen as battles to be won, reinforcing the idea that ideological opposition is insurmountable. This normalization of conflict has fostered a culture of division, where Americans are increasingly comfortable with viewing those who disagree with them as adversaries rather than fellow citizens.

The ideological clash between Trump's America First movement and woke culture has reshaped public perception in ways that have contributed to significant and lasting divisions in American society. This clash has created polarized identities, where individuals increasingly define themselves and others by their political or cultural affiliations. Media echo chambers, social media dynamics, and rising distrust in institutions have reinforced these divides, making it more difficult for Americans to find common ground.

As polarization has permeated families, communities, and institutions, the very fabric of American society has been altered. Relationships, political discourse, and social cohesion have all suffered as a result of this ideological battle, leaving Americans more divided than ever. The clash between America First and woke culture has become a defining feature of contemporary American life, raising important questions about the nation's future and the possibility of bridging these divides. Whether through efforts to foster dialogue, reform institutions, or embrace diverse perspectives, addressing this polarization will be essential for the health and unity of American society in the years to come.

Chapter 4: The Media and the Battle for Public Opinion

In-Depth Analysis of the Media's Role in Shaping and Influencing the Public's Perception of Trump and Woke Culture

The media has played a pivotal role in shaping the public's perception of both Trump's America First movement and woke culture, using its platform to frame narratives, highlight key issues, and influence how Americans interpret and react to these competing ideologies. As a powerful conduit of information, the media does more than simply report events; it selects which stories to cover, how to present them, and the language to use, all of which directly impact public perception. Through selective framing, editorial choices, and sometimes overt bias, the media has fueled the ideological clash between America First and woke culture, creating narratives that have polarized the public and reinforced divisions across society. This section provides an in-depth analysis of how the media has shaped these narratives, amplifying the conflict between these two ideologies.

Framing and Agenda-Setting: Choosing the Issues That Matter

One of the most significant ways the media shapes public perception is through agenda-setting, which involves choosing which issues to cover and, by extension, which ones to ignore. In the case of Trump and woke culture, different media outlets have focused on issues that align with their ideological leanings, creating divergent narratives that reinforce audience beliefs and values.

Conservative outlets, such as Fox News, Breitbart, and The Daily Caller, often frame Trump's America First policies as a defense of traditional American values and a necessary stand against the perceived excesses of woke culture. These outlets prioritize stories that highlight the economic and cultural threats they associate with woke policies, such as immigration and multiculturalism, which they argue weaken American sovereignty and national identity. By emphasizing these issues, conservative media outlets help reinforce a narrative of America First as a patriotic response to progressive overreach, painting Trump as a defender of American interests.

Conversely, progressive-leaning outlets like MSNBC, CNN, and The New York Times have chosen to focus on stories that underscore the potential dangers of Trump's policies, framing his America First agenda as exclusionary and even xenophobic. These outlets often highlight issues of social justice, human rights, and systemic inequality, portraying woke culture as a necessary corrective to the inequalities they associate with Trump's policies. By emphasizing issues like racial equity, LGBTQ rights, and environmental justice, progressive media aims to paint woke culture as a moral imperative and a counterbalance to what they see as Trump's regressive agenda.

The selective framing of issues contributes to a divided public perception. Audiences of conservative media are more likely to view woke culture as a threat to American values, while those who consume progressive media are more inclined to see Trump's policies as undermining civil rights and social justice. This agenda-setting effect ensures that each side of the ideological divide has a fundamentally different understanding of the same issues, making meaningful dialogue and compromise increasingly difficult.

Language and Tone: Crafting the Narrative

The language and tone used by the media play a crucial role in influencing how the public perceives both Trump and woke culture. Media outlets that support the America First agenda often use language that emphasizes strength, protection, and patriotism. Terms like "national security," "protecting American jobs," and "sovereignty" are frequently invoked to create a sense of urgency and necessity around Trump's policies. In this narrative, Trump is often described as a "fighter" or "defender" of American values, framing his actions as courageous and in the national interest.

In contrast, progressive media outlets employ language that highlights inclusivity, social justice, and human rights. Woke culture is often described with terms such as "equality," "justice," and "inclusivity," which frame it as a compassionate and forward-thinking movement. Conversely, Trump's policies are sometimes described in negative terms like "racist," "xenophobic," or "divisive." This choice of language shapes public perception by framing Trump's policies as morally questionable, while woke culture is positioned as a positive force for social progress.

The tone used by each side is also influential. Conservative media often adopt an alarmist tone when discussing woke culture, warning of the "radical left" or the dangers of "political correctness gone too far." This approach aims to evoke a sense of urgency and rally readers to protect traditional values. Progressive media, on the other hand, often adopt a tone of moral conviction when discussing social justice issues, framing woke culture as the moral high ground. By portraying themselves as champions of justice and equality, they position Trump's America First policies as a threat to vulnerable communities and societal progress.

These choices in language and tone are not merely stylistic but serve to shape public opinion in powerful ways. Readers and viewers are not only informed but also emotionally influenced, often encouraged to feel fear, anger, pride, or a sense of moral duty based on how the issues are presented. This emotive framing fosters stronger alignment with one side or the other, creating a divided media landscape where audiences are primed to view the opposing ideology with suspicion or disdain.

Selective Storytelling: Highlighting Conflicts and Controversies

The media has also played a key role in intensifying the ideological clash by focusing on conflicts and controversies that reinforce division. Stories that involve clashes between Trump supporters and progressive activists, or cases where woke culture initiatives have led to backlash, are frequently highlighted by both conservative and progressive media outlets. This selective storytelling focuses on the most divisive elements of each movement, rather than areas of potential common ground, thus reinforcing the idea that America First and woke culture are irreconcilable.

For example, conservative media outlets have frequently covered instances where woke culture initiatives—such as diversity training, renaming historical monuments, or cancel culture—have sparked public backlash. By highlighting these incidents, they create a narrative that woke culture is an overreaching and oppressive force that seeks to erase American history and punish dissenting voices. These stories are often framed as cautionary tales, warning readers of the dangers of allowing woke culture to dictate social norms.

Progressive media, in contrast, often focus on incidents where Trump supporters or America First policies have clashed with social justice movements, emphasizing cases of discrimination, intolerance, or hate crimes. By covering these incidents extensively, progressive outlets frame Trump's base as reactionary and hostile to inclusivity, portraying America First as a movement that resists social progress and threatens marginalized groups. This approach creates a sense of urgency around woke culture, positioning it as a necessary response to counteract the harm associated with America First policies.

By selectively highlighting stories that involve conflict and controversy, media outlets contribute to a perception of constant ideological warfare. This storytelling choice reinforces public perception that America First and woke culture are diametrically opposed, each side unwilling to concede or cooperate. As a result, audiences are left with an impression that these two movements are locked in an unending struggle for the future of America, further deepening polarization and entrenching ideological divisions.

Social Media's Role in Reinforcing Narratives

In addition to traditional media, social media has become a significant force in shaping public perception of Trump and woke culture. Platforms like Twitter, Facebook, and Instagram enable rapid dissemination of news and commentary, often bypassing traditional gatekeepers and amplifying extreme viewpoints. Social media allows individuals to share articles, opinions, and memes that reinforce their beliefs, creating echo chambers where users are exposed primarily to content that aligns with their ideological leanings.

For example, pro-Trump users on social media often share stories that depict woke culture as an invasive force that threatens personal freedoms and American values. These posts are often accompanied by commentary that criticizes "cancel culture," "wokeness," and "leftist extremism," creating a narrative that the America First movement is under constant attack. Hashtags like #MAGA and #AmericaFirst unite users under a shared identity, fostering a sense of community among Trump supporters who view themselves as defenders of traditional American values.

On the other side, woke culture advocates use social media to amplify issues related to social justice, systemic inequality, and human rights. Hashtags like #BlackLivesMatter, #MeToo, and #ClimateJustice create online communities that promote woke narratives and challenge conservative viewpoints. Posts on these issues often include emotionally charged language and personal stories that resonate with followers, building a shared sense of urgency and moral purpose. Social media influencers, activists, and public figures frequently contribute to these discussions, lending credibility to the woke movement and rallying support for progressive causes.

Social media's role in reinforcing narratives has led to increased polarization, as users are frequently exposed only to viewpoints that confirm their beliefs. Algorithms designed to prioritize engaging content inadvertently create echo chambers, where opposing perspectives are rarely encountered. This selective exposure has intensified ideological divides, with users increasingly viewing the other side as misguided, dangerous, or even immoral. The role of social media in shaping public perception has thus become both a driver of polarization and a force that keeps individuals insulated within their ideological bubbles.

Conclusion

The media's role in shaping public perception of Trump and woke culture has been instrumental in defining the ideological clash between these two movements. Through agenda-setting, language choices, selective storytelling, and the amplification provided by social media, media outlets have framed the conflict as a battle between two opposing forces, each vying to shape the future of America. Conservative media emphasize nationalism, tradition, and patriotism, painting woke culture as a threat to American values. Progressive media highlight social justice, inclusivity, and accountability, positioning America First policies as a regressive force that opposes progress.

This media-driven narrative has deepened divisions in American society, creating echo chambers and reinforcing polarization. Audiences on both sides are increasingly exposed to content that confirms their beliefs, intensifying their allegiance to either America First or woke culture. As a result, the media has not only reported on the ideological clash but also actively shaped and fueled it, making it a central feature of contemporary American discourse. The media's influence on public perception underscores the difficulty of finding common ground in a society where information is selectively framed, filtered, and presented in ways that amplify division.

Exploration of How Different Media Outlets (Mainstream Media vs. Alternative Media) Framed the Conflict Between Trump's Policies and Woke Ideologies

The ideological clash between Trump's America First movement and the principles of woke culture has been covered extensively across various media outlets, with stark differences in framing between mainstream and alternative media. Each type of media has approached the conflict with distinct perspectives, priorities, and rhetorical strategies, reflecting their target audiences and ideological leanings. While mainstream media largely operates within established journalistic conventions and seeks to appeal to broad audiences, alternative media often serves niche audiences and takes a more unabashedly partisan stance. This chapter explores how these two types of media have shaped the public's understanding of the ideological battle between Trump's policies and woke ideologies, revealing how each outlet has influenced perceptions of both movements.

Mainstream Media: Balancing Objectivity and Ideological Leanings

Mainstream media, which includes major news outlets such as CNN, The New York Times, Fox News, and NBC, typically strives to balance objective reporting with editorial content that reflects the organization's ideological leanings. Given their broad reach and influence, mainstream outlets have significant power to shape public opinion, and their framing of the America First and woke culture clash has been both influential and polarizing.

Progressive-Leaning Mainstream Outlets

Mainstream outlets with a progressive slant, such as CNN, The New York Times, and MSNBC, have tended to frame Trump's America First policies as regressive, divisive, and harmful to marginalized communities. Coverage in these outlets frequently highlights the social and human consequences of Trump's policies, particularly on issues like immigration, LGBTQ rights, and racial equity. By focusing on the perceived social costs of America First policies, these outlets have positioned Trump's movement as an obstacle to social justice and progress.

For instance, immigration coverage in these outlets often emphasized the humanitarian impact of Trump's border policies, including family separations and travel restrictions. Reports typically included personal stories of immigrants affected by these policies, reinforcing the view that Trump's approach was excessively punitive and lacked compassion. Similarly, stories on LGBTQ rights and gender policies highlighted the impact of Trump's policies on vulnerable populations, casting his administration as resistant to progress and inclusivity.

The tone and language used in these outlets often reinforced the idea that woke culture was a moral response to Trump's policies, with a duty to counteract what they saw as his administration's harmful effects. Woke culture was presented as a movement striving for equity and justice, positioning it as a necessary counterbalance to America First ideals. Editorials and opinion pieces frequently endorsed woke perspectives, reinforcing the idea that Trump's policies ran counter to American values of equality and inclusivity.

Conservative-Leaning Mainstream Outlets

On the other hand, mainstream outlets with a conservative leaning, such as Fox News, offered a different framing, emphasizing the America First agenda as a defense of American values, national sovereignty, and traditional culture. Coverage on Fox News often portrayed Trump as a leader who was willing to stand up against the progressive ideologies promoted by woke culture, which it framed as an attempt to transform American society in ways that disregarded the nation's heritage and values.

Fox News frequently presented stories that highlighted the perceived excesses of woke culture, from "cancel culture" incidents to debates over school curricula and historical monuments. These stories emphasized the idea that woke culture was intolerant, authoritarian, and hostile to dissenting views. Woke advocates were often depicted as an elite minority pushing their agenda on mainstream America, while Trump and his supporters were framed as the defenders of ordinary Americans.

In immigration coverage, for example, Fox News emphasized border security and the economic impact of illegal immigration on American workers. Coverage often highlighted stories of crimes committed by undocumented immigrants, supporting Trump's portrayal of immigration as a national security threat. The border wall was depicted as a symbol of American sovereignty and a protective measure against the challenges posed by unchecked immigration. In this framing, woke opposition to border policies was seen as naïve or even dangerous, representing an idealistic but unrealistic view of America's responsibilities.

Mainstream media, by virtue of its broad reach, has the power to shape large-scale public opinion, and both conservative and progressive-leaning outlets used this influence to create contrasting narratives of the America First-woke culture clash. These opposing framings, reaching millions of viewers and readers, reinforced ideological divides and contributed to the growing polarization of American society.

Alternative Media: Amplifying Partisan Narratives and Niche Ideologies

Alternative media, which includes online publications, independent podcasts, YouTube channels, and niche websites, has become a powerful force in modern discourse, particularly in its ability to engage specific ideological audiences. Without the constraints and editorial standards of mainstream media, alternative media outlets often take a more partisan approach, openly supporting one ideology and frequently using sensationalist or provocative language. Alternative media has played a crucial role in shaping perceptions of both Trump's America First policies and woke culture, often amplifying more extreme or controversial narratives that would receive less coverage in traditional news outlets.

Pro-America First Alternative Media

Pro-America First alternative media outlets, such as Breitbart, The Gateway Pundit, and conservative podcasts, have taken a strong stance in support of Trump's policies and the America First agenda. These outlets often frame woke culture as a radical, destabilizing force that seeks to undermine American traditions, erode national identity, and impose progressive ideology on the public.

For example, Breitbart frequently publishes articles that criticize woke initiatives, portraying them as overreaches that infringe on personal freedoms and cultural norms. Headlines are often provocative, aiming to capture the frustrations of their conservative audience and reinforce the idea that America First policies are necessary to protect the country from the influence of woke ideologies. Alternative media figures like Ben Shapiro and Steven Crowder have popularized this narrative, using humor, satire, and confrontational rhetoric to frame woke culture as a threat to free speech, individualism, and traditional values.

In terms of immigration, pro-America First alternative media tends to focus on stories that depict the negative impacts of immigration, such as increased crime rates or job competition. These outlets frequently feature stories that challenge mainstream narratives on immigration, arguing that woke culture promotes open borders and disregards the safety and welfare of American citizens. This framing is designed to evoke a sense of urgency and rally support for stricter immigration policies, reinforcing the idea that Trump's approach is necessary for the preservation of American security and culture.

Pro-Woke Culture Alternative Media

Alternative media outlets aligned with woke culture, such as The Young Turks, Vice News, and left-leaning podcasts, emphasize social justice issues and frequently critique Trump's policies as regressive and harmful to marginalized communities. These outlets often frame Trump's America First policies as symptomatic of a broader problem of systemic oppression, framing woke culture as a necessary response to counteract these injustices.

For instance, The Young Turks frequently covers stories related to police reform, immigration rights, and climate justice, portraying Trump's policies as aligned with corporate interests, exclusionary nationalism, and resistance to progress. In this framing, woke culture is presented as a grassroots movement that seeks to elevate marginalized voices, combat inequality, and promote a more inclusive society. Coverage often includes interviews with activists, organizers, and academics, providing context that reinforces the moral imperative of woke principles.

Pro-woke alternative media outlets also highlight incidents of discrimination, police brutality, and environmental injustice, positioning these issues as symptoms of a society that America First policies fail to address or even exacerbate. They argue that woke culture is essential to achieving systemic change, and portray America First advocates as resistant to that change out of fear, ignorance, or vested interest. This framing has a strong appeal to younger, progressive audiences, reinforcing the idea that woke culture represents the future and that Trump's policies are relics of an exclusionary past.

Alternative media outlets often use more direct, emotional language than mainstream media, fostering a sense of urgency and activism. By taking strong, unfiltered stances, alternative media plays a key role in reinforcing ideological divides, creating distinct online communities where audiences feel validated in their beliefs and are exposed to content that criticizes the opposing side.

The Impact of Contrasting Frames on Public Opinion

The stark differences in how mainstream and alternative media have framed the America First-woke culture conflict have had significant implications for public opinion. Mainstream media, with its broader reach, has helped shape widespread narratives that appeal to large segments of the population, reinforcing the perception of a binary choice between America First and woke ideologies. Alternative media, meanwhile, has provided more extreme or niche perspectives, creating ideological echo chambers where individuals can consume content that fully aligns with their worldview and dismisses opposing perspectives.

These contrasting frames have deepened polarization, making it difficult for Americans to find common ground on issues that affect society as a whole. Mainstream media has promoted this divide by presenting Trump's policies and woke culture as mutually exclusive, while alternative media has amplified the extremes of each ideology, leaving little room for moderate or nuanced viewpoints.

The framing of the America First-woke culture conflict by mainstream and alternative media has played a crucial role in shaping public opinion, reinforcing ideological divides, and intensifying polarization within American society. Mainstream media outlets have largely adhered to established ideological lines, with conservative and progressive outlets framing Trump's policies and woke culture in ways that appeal to their respective audiences. Alternative media has amplified these perspectives, often taking more extreme stances and contributing to the creation of echo chambers where audiences are increasingly insulated from opposing viewpoints.

As these contrasting narratives continue to influence public perception, they underscore the role of media as a powerful force in defining the ideological landscape. The differing portrayals of America First and woke culture by mainstream and alternative media have not only shaped individual beliefs but have also contributed to a broader cultural division that challenges the possibility of unity or compromise. This clash of frames leaves the American public with a fractured understanding of key issues, making it increasingly difficult to bridge the divides that shape contemporary society.

The Role of Social Media in Mobilizing Both Trump's Supporters and Woke Activists

Social media has become a powerful tool in the mobilization of political movements, and the ideological clash between Trump's America First supporters and woke activists has been no exception. Platforms like Twitter, Facebook, Instagram, and TikTok have transformed how political messages are shared, allowing movements to gain traction quickly and reach wide, diverse audiences. For Trump's supporters, social media provided a space to amplify the America First message, rally around Trump's policies, and challenge mainstream narratives. For woke activists, social media became a vehicle for organizing protests, promoting social justice causes, and holding individuals and institutions accountable. This section explores the role of social media in mobilizing both Trump supporters and woke activists, examining how these platforms fueled engagement, fostered community, and created a dynamic, often contentious, space for ideological confrontation.

Mobilizing Trump's Supporters: Amplifying the America First Agenda

Social media played a crucial role in rallying Trump's base around the America First agenda. Platforms like Twitter, Facebook, and alternative sites like Parler provided Trump supporters with spaces to share news, express opinions, and organize events, allowing them to bypass traditional media and reach like-minded individuals directly. Through hashtags, viral content, and influential figures, Trump's supporters used social media to strengthen their collective voice, spread pro-America First narratives, and mobilize around key political issues.

Hashtags and Rallying Cries

Hashtags like #MAGA (Make America Great Again), #AmericaFirst, and #KAG (Keep America Great) became rallying cries for Trump's supporters, creating a sense of unity and shared purpose. These hashtags allowed supporters to connect with one another, share updates, and stay informed about Trump's policies and events. By using these tags, individuals could quickly identify themselves as part of the America First movement and engage with a vast online network of supporters. This cohesion on social media fostered a powerful sense of identity and solidarity among Trump's base, reinforcing their loyalty and dedication to his agenda.

Hashtags also provided a way for Trump's supporters to amplify specific issues and create momentum around them. For instance, during debates over border security and the construction of a border wall, hashtags like #BuildTheWall and #SecureOurBorders gained traction, signaling widespread support for these policies and placing pressure on lawmakers. The visibility of these hashtags allowed Trump's supporters to frame immigration as a national security issue, shaping public discourse and demonstrating the influence of social media in mobilizing public opinion around America First ideals.

Memes, Viral Content, and Influencers

Memes, videos, and other shareable content became essential tools for mobilizing Trump's supporters. Memes often featured satirical takes on political issues, casting Trump as a hero or warrior against "leftist" or "globalist" forces, while portraying woke culture as out of touch or dangerous. These images and videos not only entertained Trump's base but also provided them with easily digestible, shareable content that reinforced their beliefs and spread America First narratives.

Influential social media figures, such as conservative commentators and political personalities, played a significant role in disseminating pro-Trump content. Figures like Ben Shapiro,

Dan Bongino, and Candace Owens used their platforms to discuss America First policies, counter woke narratives, and mobilize followers around key issues. These influencers created a feedback loop, where they echoed Trump's talking points, energized their followers, and reinforced the collective identity of Trump's supporters as defenders of American values.

Organizing and Coordinating Events

Social media was instrumental in coordinating Trump rallies, gatherings, and even protests. Platforms like Facebook and Twitter allowed organizers to share event details, communicate logistical information, and rally participants. Pro-Trump rallies often utilized social media not only for promotion but also to create a sense of excitement and urgency, framing these gatherings as opportunities to "show support" for Trump and push back against woke culture.

During the 2020 election and the COVID-19 pandemic, social media became a primary tool for organizing protests against perceived government overreach and promoting "Stop the Steal" events, which questioned the legitimacy of the election results. Social media allowed Trump's supporters to organize quickly, mobilize large groups, and challenge narratives from mainstream media or government officials. This online mobilization underscored the power of social media as a tool for collective action, amplifying the voices of Trump's supporters and their commitment to America First values.

Mobilizing Woke Activists: Advancing Social Justice and Accountability

For woke activists, social media provided a platform to advocate for social justice, amplify marginalized voices, and hold individuals and institutions accountable for systemic injustices. Platforms like Twitter, Instagram, and TikTok became digital arenas for woke culture, where hashtags, viral posts, and influencer-led campaigns helped draw attention to issues like racial inequality, gender rights, and environmental justice. Through online mobilization, woke activists were able to quickly raise awareness, organize protests, and build a sense of community around progressive causes.

Hashtag Activism and Digital Campaigns

Hashtags like #BlackLivesMatter, #MeToo, and #ClimateJustice became central to the woke movement, allowing activists to organize digital campaigns that resonated globally. These hashtags helped bring attention to specific issues, from police brutality and sexual harassment to climate change and environmental justice. Each hashtag created a virtual space where individuals could share personal stories, data, and calls to action, making social media a powerful tool for advocacy.

Hashtag activism allowed woke culture to frame social justice issues in a way that was easily accessible and widely shareable. For instance, #BlackLivesMatter posts often featured videos of protests, testimonies from affected communities, and educational resources on systemic racism. These posts encouraged people to participate in discussions, sign petitions, donate to causes, and join local protests. By using social media to organize around specific hashtags, woke activists created a movement that was as much online as it was offline, using digital tools to reach audiences beyond traditional activist circles.

Viral Stories and Accountability

Social media has empowered woke activists to hold public figures, institutions, and companies accountable for actions and statements perceived as discriminatory, exploitative, or unethical. Viral stories, often fueled by videos, screenshots, or leaked information, allowed woke activists to highlight injustices and push for accountability. This practice, sometimes referred to as "cancel culture," involved boycotts, online petitions, and widespread criticism directed at individuals or organizations deemed to have violated progressive principles.

The #MeToo movement is a prime example of how social media was used to hold people accountable. By sharing personal experiences of sexual harassment and assault, individuals were able to expose pervasive issues in the entertainment industry, politics, and beyond. Social media enabled these stories to reach a massive audience, sparking a wave of activism that led to policy changes, resignations, and a broader societal reckoning. This approach to accountability reinforced woke culture's focus on social justice, using social media as a tool to address long-standing issues and demand tangible change.

Organizing Protests and Direct Action

Social media has proven invaluable for woke activists in organizing protests, marches, and other forms of direct action. Platforms like Twitter and Instagram allow activists to coordinate logistics, share rally points, and communicate real-time updates, making it easier for large groups to mobilize quickly and effectively. The Black Lives Matter protests in 2020 exemplified how social media can transform local activism into a global movement, with protests occurring in cities across the United States and around the world.

These platforms also served as tools for educating and preparing participants, with posts that shared protest guidelines, legal rights, and strategies for de-escalation. Woke activists used social media to foster a sense of solidarity and purpose, emphasizing the importance of collective action in confronting systemic injustices. By leveraging social media's connectivity, woke culture advocates were able to reach wide audiences and inspire activism on a global scale.

The Role of Algorithms and Echo Chambers in Reinforcing Ideologies

The mobilizing power of social media is amplified by algorithms that prioritize engagement, often leading users to content that aligns with their existing beliefs. This tendency creates "echo chambers," where individuals are exposed primarily to views that confirm their opinions and reinforce their sense of belonging to a particular movement. For both Trump's supporters and woke activists, these echo chambers intensify loyalty to their respective ideologies and deepen their commitment to advancing their causes.

Echo Chambers for Trump's Supporters

Social media algorithms have created spaces where Trump's supporters are primarily exposed to pro-America First content, reinforcing their beliefs and intensifying their commitment to the movement. Platforms like Parler, which catered specifically to conservative users, exemplified this phenomenon, offering a space where Trump supporters could discuss politics without encountering opposing viewpoints. This environment allowed for the unchecked spread of America First narratives, leading supporters to feel validated in their beliefs and increasingly isolated from woke perspectives.

Echo Chambers for Woke Activists

For woke activists, platforms like Twitter and Instagram create similar echo chambers, where users primarily engage with content that supports social justice and progressive ideals. Woke culture thrives in these spaces, with users sharing stories, hashtags, and viral posts that reinforce shared values. These echo chambers build solidarity among woke activists, fostering a sense of community and shared responsibility to advocate for change.

While these echo chambers strengthen the movements, they also contribute to polarization by limiting exposure to alternative viewpoints. For both Trump supporters and woke activists, social media has created ideological silos that make it difficult to bridge divides or engage in constructive dialogue.

Social media has played a transformative role in mobilizing both Trump's supporters and woke activists, providing platforms where each group can amplify its message, organize events, and build a sense of collective identity. For Trump's base, social media has served as a space to rally around the America First agenda, challenge woke culture, and bypass traditional media. For woke activists, social media has been a powerful tool for advancing social justice, holding individuals accountable, and organizing protests.

The role of algorithms and echo chambers has further intensified this mobilization, creating environments where individuals are continually exposed to content that reinforces their beliefs. While social media has empowered both movements, it has also contributed to polarization by fostering ideological silos. The mobilizing power of social media underscores its double-edged nature: it unites people around shared causes but also deepens the divides that characterize contemporary American society.

The proliferation of misinformation, fake news, and echo chambers has significantly deepened the cultural divide between Trump's America First supporters and proponents of woke culture. In an era characterized by information overload and the rapid dissemination of content through digital platforms, distinguishing fact from fiction has become increasingly challenging. This environment has allowed misleading information to flourish, shaping public opinion in ways that reinforce existing beliefs and exacerbate societal polarization. This subchapter explores how misinformation and echo chambers have contributed to the widening gap between these two ideological camps, undermining trust in traditional institutions and complicating efforts to find common ground.

The Rise of Misinformation and Fake News

The advent of the internet and social media has democratized information sharing, enabling anyone with an internet connection to publish content that can reach a global audience. While this has positive implications for freedom of expression, it has also led to the spread of misinformation and fake news—deliberately fabricated or misleading content presented as legitimate news. These false narratives often play into the biases and fears of specific audiences, making them more likely to be accepted and shared without verification.

1, Misinformation Targeting Trump Supporters

Among Trump's America First supporters, misinformation has often centered around themes of nationalism, distrust of the establishment, and skepticism toward mainstream media. Conspiracy theories such as QAnon gained traction within certain segments of Trump's base, promoting unfounded claims about government corruption and elite cabals. False narratives about election fraud in the 2020 presidential election were widely circulated, leading many to question the legitimacy of the electoral process despite a lack of evidence. This misinformation reinforced beliefs that Trump was a victim of a concerted effort by political opponents and the media to undermine his presidency.

The spread of such misinformation was facilitated by social media platforms and alternative news sites that catered to conservative audiences. Algorithms that prioritize engagement often promoted sensational or controversial content, regardless of its accuracy. As a result, false stories could rapidly gain visibility, shaping perceptions and fueling distrust in institutions like the media, the judiciary, and electoral systems.

2. Misinformation Affecting Woke Activists

Woke activists were not immune to misinformation either. Fake news targeting this group often involved exaggerated or misleading reports about incidents of injustice, which, while drawing attention to genuine issues, sometimes lacked factual accuracy. For instance, stories might circulate about events of police brutality or discrimination that were later found to be misrepresented. While the intention behind sharing such stories was often to highlight systemic problems, the use of inaccurate information risked undermining the credibility of the broader movement.

Additionally, misinformation aimed at discrediting woke culture circulated widely. False claims about policies like defunding the police or implementing socialist agendas were amplified to provoke fear and resistance among those opposed to progressive changes. These narratives often misrepresented the goals and methods of woke activists, contributing to misunderstandings and heightened tensions between opposing groups.

The Role of Echo Chambers in Reinforcing Beliefs

Echo chambers—environments where individuals are exposed predominantly to opinions and information that align with their existing beliefs—have become more prevalent with the rise of personalized content algorithms on social media platforms. These algorithms curate content based on user behavior, creating a feedback loop that reinforces one's viewpoints and filters out dissenting perspectives.

1. Echo Chambers Among Trump Supporters

For many America First advocates, echo chambers solidified their support for Trump and skepticism toward opposing viewpoints. By engaging primarily with like-minded individuals and sources, these supporters received a steady stream of content that validated their beliefs about issues like immigration, national security, and cultural identity. Echo chambers amplified messages that portrayed Trump as a champion against corrupt elites and a protector of traditional American values.

The isolation from alternative perspectives made it difficult for new information to challenge established beliefs. When confronted with contradictory evidence or viewpoints, individuals within these echo chambers were more likely to dismiss them as biased or false, further entrenching their positions. This environment also facilitated the spread of misinformation, as false narratives went unchallenged within the group.

1. Echo Chambers Among Woke Activists

Similarly, woke activists often operated within echo chambers that reinforced their perspectives on social justice, systemic inequality, and cultural change. Engaging with content and communities that shared their commitment to progressive values, activists received continual affirmation of their views. While this fostered solidarity and collective action, it also sometimes limited exposure to constructive criticism or alternative approaches to addressing societal issues.

The echo chamber effect could lead to the amplification of extreme viewpoints or strategies that might not resonate with broader audiences. Additionally, the lack of engagement with dissenting opinions sometimes resulted in misunderstandings about the motivations and concerns of those outside the movement, hindering opportunities for dialogue and collaboration.

The Erosion of Trust in Traditional Media and Institutions

The prevalence of misinformation and the reinforcement of beliefs within echo chambers have contributed to a growing distrust of traditional media and institutions. Both America First supporters and woke activists have expressed skepticism toward mainstream news outlets, albeit for different reasons.

1. Distrust Among Trump Supporters

Trump frequently characterized mainstream media as "fake news" and the "enemy of the people," rhetoric that resonated with his supporters who felt that their perspectives were misrepresented or ignored by established news organizations. This distrust was exacerbated by instances where media coverage appeared biased or dismissive of conservative viewpoints. As a result, many turned to alternative media sources that aligned with their beliefs, further isolating them from mainstream narratives.

The erosion of trust extended to governmental institutions perceived as part of the establishment. Investigations into the Trump administration, judicial rulings, and actions by federal agencies were often viewed with suspicion, seen as efforts by entrenched powers to resist change. This skepticism made it challenging to establish common facts or authorities that could bridge the divide between differing viewpoints.

1. Distrust Among Woke Activists

Woke activists also harbored distrust toward traditional media and institutions, criticizing them for perpetuating systemic biases and failing to adequately address issues of inequality and injustice. Mainstream media was often seen as catering to corporate interests or lacking diversity in representation and perspectives. This perception led activists to rely on independent media outlets, social media platforms, and grassroots networks for information and organization.

The skepticism extended to governmental and legal institutions, which activists argued were structured in ways that maintained systemic oppression. High-profile incidents of police brutality, racial discrimination, and economic inequality reinforced the belief that traditional institutions were resistant to necessary reforms. This distrust motivated activists to push for significant systemic changes, sometimes outside the established political processes.

The Polarizing Effect on Public Discourse

The combination of misinformation, echo chambers, and eroding trust in traditional institutions has had a polarizing effect on public discourse. With each side operating from different sets of "facts" and narratives, finding common ground has become increasingly difficult.

1. Challenges to Constructive Dialogue

The spread of misinformation creates a fragmented reality where basic agreements on facts are lacking. Without a shared understanding of events or data, debates often devolve into exchanges of accusations and denials rather than productive discussions. This fragmentation hinders the ability to address complex societal issues collaboratively, as stakeholders cannot even agree on the nature of the problems or the validity of proposed solutions.

2, Amplification of Extremism

Echo chambers can also contribute to the radicalization of viewpoints. As individuals are exposed only to reinforcing content, more extreme ideas can gain traction without the moderating influence of diverse perspectives. This phenomenon can lead to the normalization of fringe beliefs and a willingness to consider or endorse actions that would have previously been unacceptable.

3.Undermining Democratic Processes

The pervasive distrust and polarization fueled by misinformation and echo chambers threaten the foundations of democratic society. When large segments of the population question the legitimacy of elections, the integrity of institutions, or the validity of the media, the social cohesion necessary for democracy is weakened. This environment can lead to increased social unrest, decreased civic engagement, and vulnerability to manipulation by bad actors seeking to exploit divisions for their own gain.

Efforts to Combat Misinformation and Bridge Divides

Recognizing the dangers posed by misinformation and echo chambers, various stakeholders have initiated efforts to address these challenges.

1, Media Literacy Initiatives

Educational programs aimed at improving media literacy seek to equip individuals with the skills to critically evaluate information sources, identify biases, and discern credible news from falsehoods. By fostering critical thinking, these initiatives aim to reduce the spread of misinformation and encourage more informed public discourse.

2, Platform Responsibility

Social media companies have come under increasing pressure to address the role their platforms play in disseminating misinformation. Measures such as content moderation policies, fact-checking labels, and algorithm adjustments have been implemented to varying degrees. However, these efforts often face criticism from both sides—America First supporters may view them as censorship targeting conservative voices, while woke activists may argue they are insufficient or unevenly applied.

3.Promoting Dialogue

Some organizations and community leaders are working to create spaces for constructive dialogue between opposing groups. By facilitating conversations that emphasize listening and understanding, these initiatives aim to bridge divides and find common ground on shared concerns. While challenging, such efforts are crucial in rebuilding trust and fostering cooperation across ideological lines.

Conclusion

The impact of misinformation, fake news, and echo chambers has significantly deepened the cultural divide between Trump's America First movement and woke culture advocates. These factors have distorted public perception, reinforced existing biases, and eroded trust in media and institutions, making constructive dialogue and mutual understanding increasingly elusive. Addressing these challenges requires concerted efforts from individuals, media organizations, technology platforms, and society at large to promote media literacy, encourage critical thinking, and foster open, respectful communication. Only by confronting the issues of misinformation and polarization can the cultural divide be bridged, allowing for collaborative solutions to the complex problems facing the nation.

Chapter 5: Corporate America in the Crossfire

How Corporate America Became a Battleground for the Ideological Conflict Between Trump's America First Agenda and Woke Politics

In recent years, corporate America has found itself caught in the crossfire of the ideological clash between Trump's America First agenda and the principles of woke politics. While corporations have historically avoided taking explicit political stances, the rise of social media, consumer activism, and shifting cultural expectations have compelled businesses to engage with controversial social and political issues. For many companies, these pressures have created a complex and often uncomfortable balancing act, as they attempt to satisfy consumers, shareholders, and employees with conflicting expectations. This chapter explores how corporate America became a key battleground for the ideological struggle between the America First movement and woke politics, examining the pressures, consequences, and implications of corporate involvement in this cultural war.

The Rise of Consumer Activism and Brand Expectations

One of the primary forces driving corporations into the ideological fray has been the rise of consumer activism, where individuals increasingly expect companies to take clear stances on social and political issues. This trend is particularly strong among younger consumers, who prioritize values-driven brands and demand accountability from companies regarding their social impact. As a result, corporations are now expected not only to sell products but to demonstrate their commitment to causes such as diversity, sustainability, and social justice.

1.Pressure from Woke Politics

Woke politics emphasizes inclusivity, social justice, and accountability, and many activists and consumers who identify with woke principles expect companies to align with these values. For example, consumers may demand that a brand take a public stand on issues such as LGBTQ rights, racial justice, climate change, or gender equality. Brands that remain silent on these issues are often criticized for failing to support progress, while those that take an explicit stance are praised for their social responsibility.

This pressure has led many companies to incorporate woke values into their public messaging and business practices. For instance, major corporations have adopted diversity and inclusion programs, released statements in support of the Black Lives Matter movement, and launched initiatives to reduce their environmental impact. By doing so, these companies aim to demonstrate their commitment to social justice, appealing to consumers who prioritize ethical considerations in their purchasing decisions.

2.Pushback from America First Advocates

While woke consumers advocate for corporate alignment with progressive values, America First supporters often view these actions as an unwanted intrusion of politics into the business world. From their perspective, corporate alignment with woke politics is seen as pandering to progressive ideologies that undermine traditional American values. This sentiment is particularly strong among conservatives who argue that corporations should focus on providing quality products and services rather than engaging in cultural or political debates.

The backlash from America First advocates has led to calls for boycotts against companies that align with woke values, with consumers choosing to support brands they believe reflect their own values. For example, boycotts of companies that publicly supported LGBTQ rights or policies addressing racial inequality became prominent within conservative circles, with some America First advocates even promoting alternatives to "woke" brands. This tension has placed corporate America in a difficult position, as companies are forced to navigate the potential for backlash from both sides of the ideological spectrum.

High-Profile Examples: Corporations in the Crosshairs

Several high-profile cases have highlighted the complexities and risks of corporate involvement in the cultural war between America First and woke politics. These examples illustrate how corporations, whether by choice or external pressure, can find themselves at the center of ideological controversies.

1.Nike and the Colin Kaepernick Campaign

One of the most prominent examples of a brand aligning with woke politics is Nike's decision to feature former NFL player Colin Kaepernick in its 2018 advertising campaign. Kaepernick, who famously kneeled during the national anthem to protest police brutality, had become a polarizing figure, with many America First advocates viewing his actions as unpatriotic. Nike's campaign, which included the tagline "Believe in something. Even if it means sacrificing everything," was a clear endorsement of Kaepernick's activism.

While the campaign resonated strongly with consumers who supported woke ideals of social justice and protest, it provoked an intense backlash from conservative groups and America First supporters who accused Nike of promoting anti-American sentiments. The campaign led to calls for boycotts, with some critics even posting videos of themselves burning Nike products in protest. Despite the controversy, Nike's sales surged, demonstrating the growing influence of values-driven consumer behavior and the potential rewards for companies that align with woke values, even in the face of conservative backlash.

2.Chick-fil-A and Conservative Values

In contrast, Chick-fil-A has long been associated with conservative values, particularly in its support of traditional family structures and Christian principles. The company's history of donations to organizations that oppose same-sex marriage led to widespread criticism from progressive activists and calls for boycotts from LGBTQ rights groups. While Chick-fil-A has since modified its charitable giving policies, its reputation as a conservative, family-oriented brand persists.

Chick-fil-A's positioning attracted strong support from America First advocates who saw the company as a defender of traditional values amid growing pressure from woke activists. The company's stance became a rallying point for conservatives, with many patrons choosing to support Chick-fil-A in a symbolic rejection of woke influence on corporate policies. This example highlights how aligning with conservative values can create brand loyalty among America First supporters, while also provoking ongoing opposition from progressive consumers.

3.Disney and the 'Don't Say Gay' Bill Controversy

The Walt Disney Company became embroiled in controversy over its response to Florida's Parental Rights in Education Act, which critics dubbed the "Don't Say Gay" bill. Initially, Disney faced backlash from woke activists and employees for its perceived silence on the legislation, which restricted discussions of sexual orientation and gender identity in certain school settings. Under pressure, Disney ultimately took a public stance against the bill, pledging support for LGBTQ rights.

This decision led to a swift backlash from conservative groups and America First supporters, who accused Disney of promoting a progressive agenda that undermined parental rights and traditional family values. Some conservative politicians even proposed retaliatory measures, such as revoking Disney's special tax status in Florida. The Disney controversy exemplifies the challenges faced by corporations in navigating the expectations of woke consumers and activists while contending with opposition from conservative groups who view these actions as ideological overreach.

The Influence of Social Media on Corporate Positioning

Social media has amplified the impact of consumer expectations, enabling both woke activists and America First supporters to pressure companies more directly and publicly. Through platforms like Twitter, Instagram, and Facebook, consumers can instantly voice their support or outrage, often leading to viral campaigns that influence corporate behavior. Social media has effectively transformed consumers into stakeholders with the power to impact brand reputation and even sales.

1.The Speed of Social Media Backlash

In the age of social media, corporations must contend with the speed at which public backlash can erupt. A single statement or perceived misstep can spark widespread criticism within hours, with hashtags and trending topics drawing even more attention to the issue. This rapid escalation leaves companies with little time to craft responses, often forcing them to choose sides in the America First versus woke culture debate.

For example, after a company releases a statement on a social issue, social media users can quickly amplify supportive or critical voices, with both woke activists and America First advocates weighing in. The speed and intensity of these reactions compel companies to adopt clearer positions, as neutrality becomes increasingly difficult to maintain under scrutiny.

2.Direct Pressure from Influencers and Activists

Social media influencers and activists play a major role in pressuring companies to take a stand. Influencers with large followings can mobilize support or opposition, influencing how brands are perceived by a broad audience. Woke activists often leverage social media to call for boycotts or demand accountability from corporations, while conservative influencers may rally their followers to support brands that resist woke pressures.

This direct pressure can compel companies to make public statements, issue apologies, or alter their policies to appease their audiences. However, doing so often invites backlash from the opposing side, demonstrating the precarious position that corporate America occupies in the face of polarized public opinion.

The Business Dilemma: Balancing Profit with Principles

The clash between America First and woke politics has created a dilemma for corporate America, as companies strive to balance profit motives with the expectations of an increasingly values-driven consumer base. While aligning with woke values can boost brand loyalty among progressive consumers, it can alienate conservative customers, and vice versa. Many companies now face the challenge of crafting policies and messaging that appeal to diverse, often conflicting audiences.

1.Adopting a Selective Approach

Some corporations have opted to adopt a selective approach, supporting specific causes that align with their brand identity while avoiding more contentious issues. For instance, a company may support environmental sustainability but refrain from commenting on political or social debates. This strategy allows companies to demonstrate social responsibility without wading too deeply into the America First-woke culture conflict. However, selective engagement can also provoke criticism from activists who expect comprehensive commitment to progressive causes.

2,The Shift Toward Corporate Social Responsibility

The cultural clash has accelerated the trend of Corporate Social Responsibility (CSR), where businesses integrate social, environmental, and ethical considerations into their operations. Companies are now expected not only to generate profits but to contribute positively to society. However, CSR is often interpreted differently by America First advocates and woke activists, with each side emphasizing different priorities.

For woke consumers, CSR means taking active stances on issues like diversity, climate change, and gender equality. For America First supporters, CSR should focus on job creation, supporting American workers, and preserving traditional values. This divergence in expectations underscores the difficulty companies face in attempting to satisfy both constituencies, as actions that appeal to one group may alienate the other.

Corporate America has become a key battleground in the ideological conflict between Trump's America First agenda and woke politics. As consumer expectations evolve and social media amplifies the voices of both woke activists and America First supporters, companies find themselves under unprecedented pressure to take stances on complex social issues. This shift has placed corporations in a difficult position, as they attempt to balance profit motives with conflicting values and public expectations.

The rise of consumer activism and the polarization of public opinion have made neutrality nearly impossible, forcing companies to navigate a minefield of cultural and political expectations. As corporate America continues to respond to these pressures, its actions will likely remain a reflection of the broader ideological clash, highlighting the extent to which social and political values have permeated even the world of business. The role of corporations in this ideological battleground underscores the challenges and complexities of operating in a society increasingly divided along cultural lines, where the stakes of corporate decisions go beyond profits and into the realm of national identity, values, and ethics.

Analysis of Specific Cases Where Companies Took a Stance on Social Justice Issues, Facing Backlash or Support from Different Segments of Society

In recent years, companies taking public stances on social justice issues have found themselves at the center of controversy, facing both backlash and support from polarized segments of society. With rising consumer expectations for brands to demonstrate corporate responsibility and values alignment, many companies have been compelled to navigate complex social and political landscapes. This subchapter explores specific cases where corporations took stands on social justice issues, examining the public responses they faced from both supporters and critics, and the broader implications of these decisions on their brand reputations and business outcomes.

Nike and Colin Kaepernick: A Polarizing Campaign on Social Justice

Nike's 2018 campaign featuring former NFL player Colin Kaepernick was a watershed moment for corporate activism and a defining example of how brands can become entangled in the ideological divide between woke politics and America First supporters. Kaepernick, who had kneeled during the national anthem to protest police brutality and racial injustice, had become a controversial figure, celebrated by some for his activism and criticized by others for what they viewed as disrespect to the flag and national identity.

Nike's Decision and the Campaign

Nike's decision to make Kaepernick the face of its "Just Do It" campaign marked a bold move in support of social justice and the right to protest. With the tagline "Believe in something. Even if it means sacrificing everything," the campaign highlighted Kaepernick's personal and professional sacrifices for his cause. Nike's message was a clear alignment with progressive values of activism and social responsibility, demonstrating a willingness to engage with controversial issues.

Public Backlash and Support

The campaign received an overwhelmingly polarized response. America First advocates and conservative critics accused Nike of pandering to woke culture and betraying American values, with some consumers even burning their Nike products in protest. Social media was flooded with calls for boycotts, with #BoycottNike trending as conservative commentators and influencers voiced their disapproval. They argued that Nike was promoting anti-American sentiments and disrespecting the military and law enforcement.

However, Nike's campaign also resonated strongly with woke activists and younger, progressive consumers who viewed Kaepernick's activism as courageous and necessary. For these supporters, Nike's stance was a refreshing break from corporate neutrality, showing a commitment to values that aligned with their own beliefs in social justice. The campaign was widely celebrated on social media by supporters of Kaepernick's cause, and Nike saw a notable increase in brand loyalty among progressive audiences.

Business Outcome

Despite the backlash, Nike's bold move ultimately paid off. The company experienced a boost in online sales and stock performance, as the campaign resonated with a younger demographic that values social activism. By taking a calculated risk, Nike was able to solidify its brand identity as socially conscious and willing to address difficult issues, even if it alienated some of its conservative consumers. This case demonstrated that, while corporate activism carries risks, brands willing to take a clear stand can strengthen their appeal with target audiences.

Gillette's "The Best Men Can Be" Campaign: Addressing Toxic Masculinity

Gillette's 2019 ad campaign, titled "The Best Men Can Be," took aim at toxic masculinity, calling on men to challenge bullying, harassment, and other harmful behaviors. The campaign was launched in response to the #MeToo movement and was part of Gillette's effort to address shifting societal expectations around masculinity and gender roles.

Campaign Message and Intent

The ad depicted scenes of men intervening in situations of bullying and harassment, advocating for a more compassionate, respectful model of masculinity. Gillette framed the campaign as an evolution of its long-standing tagline, "The Best a Man Can Get," encouraging men to uphold positive values and challenge stereotypes. Gillette's message was intended to align the brand with progressive attitudes toward gender equality and social responsibility.

Reactions: Polarized Responses

The campaign received a polarized response. Progressive audiences generally praised Gillette for addressing a complex issue and encouraging men to reflect on societal expectations. Advocates for gender equality welcomed the campaign as a constructive message on redefining masculinity and challenging harmful norms. Social media users shared the ad widely, applauding Gillette's support of the #MeToo movement and its willingness to address a difficult topic.

However, the ad also sparked significant backlash, particularly from conservative groups and some America First advocates who viewed it as an attack on traditional masculinity. Critics argued that the campaign was "anti-male" and a product of woke culture, accusing Gillette of virtue signaling and alienating its core male demographic. Some consumers called for boycotts, expressing frustration over what they saw as corporate overreach into personal and cultural issues.

Business Outcome

Gillette's campaign had mixed business results. While the ad generated extensive media coverage and strengthened brand loyalty among progressive consumers, the backlash from conservative groups impacted the company's reputation among some long-time customers. Though Gillette maintained its commitment to the campaign's message, the polarized reactions underscored the risks associated with taking a clear stance on divisive social issues. This case highlighted the balancing act that corporations face in addressing cultural topics without alienating segments of their consumer base.

Starbucks and Racial Bias Training: Navigating a Crisis with a Woke Response

In 2018, Starbucks faced a public relations crisis when two Black men were arrested at a Philadelphia store while waiting for a friend, sparking allegations of racial profiling. In response, Starbucks took a highly publicized step toward addressing racial bias within its organization, closing over 8,000 stores for an afternoon to conduct racial bias training for employees.

Starbucks' Response

Starbucks CEO Kevin Johnson issued an apology and acknowledged the need for systemic change within the company.

The decision to close thousands of stores for racial bias training was unprecedented and positioned Starbucks as a company committed to addressing racial issues proactively. The training was designed to increase awareness of unconscious bias and foster a more inclusive environment for customers and employees.

Support and Backlash

The decision was met with widespread praise from woke activists and social justice advocates, who saw Starbucks' response as a sincere attempt to address racial bias and promote inclusivity. Many commended the company for acknowledging its shortcomings and taking immediate, concrete action to make amends. Starbucks' efforts were widely covered in the media, and the incident and its response became a high-profile example of corporate accountability.

However, some conservative voices criticized the move as unnecessary and reactionary, arguing that Starbucks was giving in to woke pressures. Critics suggested that the incident was isolated and did not warrant a company-wide response, viewing the racial bias training as an overreaction that pandered to progressive sensibilities. These critics saw the move as part of a broader trend of corporate virtue signaling that they felt undermined the company's business objectives.

Outcome

Starbucks' decision to engage in racial bias training ultimately helped to restore its public image among progressive consumers, positioning the company as socially aware and responsive to social justice concerns. While some conservative consumers remained critical, Starbucks' proactive approach allowed it to turn a potentially damaging incident into an opportunity to align with its brand values of inclusivity and corporate responsibility. This case underscored the potential benefits of aligning with woke values in times of crisis, even at the risk of alienating more conservative consumers.

Walmart and Gun Sales: Balancing Safety Concerns with Consumer Expectations

In 2019, following a mass shooting at a Walmart store in El Paso, Texas, Walmart announced significant changes to its policies on gun and ammunition sales. The company decided to stop selling certain types of ammunition and requested that customers refrain from openly carrying firearms in stores, even in states where open carry was permitted.

Walmart's Policy Changes

Walmart's new policies aimed to address growing concerns about gun violence and promote a safer shopping environment. The decision came amid increasing pressure on corporations to address gun control and adopt policies that promote public safety. Walmart's stance was an attempt to balance consumer safety concerns with respect for gun rights in states where open carry laws are common.

Support and Opposition

Progressive activists and gun control advocates praised Walmart's decision as a positive step toward reducing gun violence, applauding the company's willingness to take action in the absence of federal policy changes. For many supporters, Walmart's stance represented a corporate commitment to public safety and responsible business practices.

On the other hand, America First advocates and pro-gun rights supporters criticized Walmart's policies as a capitulation to woke culture and an infringement on Second Amendment rights. Conservative groups argued that Walmart was undermining lawful gun owners' rights and turning its back on rural, conservative customers who view gun ownership as part of their identity. The backlash included calls for boycotts, with some conservative consumers pledging to shop at stores that upheld open-carry policies.

Outcome

Walmart's decision reflected the challenges of navigating politically sensitive issues within a diverse consumer base. While the policy change garnered support from progressive audiences, it also risked alienating conservative customers. By taking a cautious but clear stance on gun control, Walmart signaled a commitment to safety without fully aligning itself with either side of the gun rights debate. This case illustrates the balancing act that corporations face when addressing issues that intersect with deeply held cultural and political values.

The cases of Nike, Gillette, Starbucks, and Walmart highlight the complexities corporations face when taking stances on social justice issues in a polarized society. Each company's decision to address controversial topics resulted in both support and backlash, illustrating the challenges of navigating consumer expectations while managing brand reputation. For many brands, taking a stand on social justice issues is a double-edged sword: while aligning with woke values can strengthen relationships with progressive consumers, it often provokes criticism from conservative groups aligned with America First ideals.

These examples underscore the delicate balance that corporate America must strike in today's politically charged environment, where even well-intentioned actions can be interpreted as endorsements of one ideology over another. As companies continue to grapple with these issues, the cases explored here serve as a reminder of the risks and rewards involved in corporate activism, and the challenges of maintaining brand integrity in the face of an ideologically divided consumer base.

The Impact of Corporate Activism on Business Practices, Consumer Behavior, and the Broader Economy

Corporate activism—when companies take public stances on social, political, and environmental issues—has transformed business practices, consumer behavior, and even aspects of the broader economy. As companies increasingly respond to the demands of values-driven consumers, they have shifted their operational and marketing approaches to align with the principles of corporate social responsibility. While this evolution has reinforced brand loyalty among certain consumer segments, it has also provoked backlash, creating new dynamics in the marketplace and influencing economic trends. This chapter explores the impact of corporate activism across these domains, examining both the benefits and challenges it presents for businesses, consumers, and the economy as a whole.

The Transformation of Business Practices Through Corporate Activism

Corporate activism has pushed companies to go beyond traditional business practices, incorporating social and political considerations into their operational strategies. From supply chain management and hiring practices to marketing campaigns and community engagement, companies are now expected to align their practices with specific values that resonate with their target audiences.

Integrating Social Responsibility into Operations

As corporate activism has gained prominence, companies have adopted policies that emphasize ethical practices in their operations. For example, many companies have implemented diversity and inclusion programs, environmental sustainability measures, and community outreach initiatives. Corporations like Patagonia and Ben & Jerry's have championed social causes as part of their core identity, incorporating these values into their product sourcing, employee policies, and philanthropic efforts.

Such initiatives can strengthen brand identity and foster loyalty among consumers who prioritize corporate responsibility. However, they also pose logistical and financial challenges, as ethical sourcing and sustainable practices can be more expensive than conventional methods. Companies must therefore balance their commitment to activism with profitability, sometimes passing on higher costs to consumers or absorbing them in an effort to maintain competitive pricing.

Adjusting Marketing and Branding to Reflect Values

Corporate activism has led to a shift in how brands market themselves, with many incorporating social and political messaging into their campaigns. For instance, brands often use advertising to highlight their stances on issues like racial equality, gender rights, or environmental sustainability. These campaigns not only promote products but also signal the brand's alignment with the values of woke culture or, in some cases, traditional values favored by America First supporters.

While this values-based marketing has succeeded in building stronger connections with certain consumer demographics, it also risks alienating other segments. Brands that lean too heavily into woke or America First messaging may inadvertently narrow their appeal, making it difficult to attract a diverse customer base. This polarization in branding strategies reflects the broader ideological divides within society and highlights the challenges businesses face in navigating complex cultural dynamics.

Shaping Internal Policies to Reflect Public Commitments

To align with public stances on social justice or cultural issues, many companies have adjusted internal policies to reflect their corporate activism. For example, tech companies like Google and Microsoft have implemented programs to increase workforce diversity and address pay equity. Similarly, some companies have introduced environmental targets, such as carbon neutrality or waste reduction, to demonstrate their commitment to sustainability.

These changes influence not only public perception but also employee morale and corporate culture. Employees are increasingly expecting their employers to reflect progressive values, with some even seeking out companies known for their activism. However, these internal policies also bring challenges, as companies may face backlash from employees or external groups that disagree with their stances, leading to potential tension within the workplace.

Shifts in Consumer Behavior in Response to Corporate Activism

Corporate activism has significantly influenced consumer behavior, as individuals increasingly make purchasing decisions based on alignment with their personal values. This trend is particularly strong among younger generations, who prioritize ethical considerations and are more likely to engage with companies that reflect their social and political beliefs. However, this values-driven consumption has also led to a divide in the marketplace, as consumers reward companies that align with their views while actively avoiding or boycotting those that don't.

The Rise of Values-Driven Consumers

For many consumers, especially Millennials and Generation Z, corporate alignment with social causes is a factor in purchasing decisions. These consumers often research a brand's stance on issues like environmental impact, labor practices, and social justice before making purchases. Brands like TOMS, which donates a portion of its profits to social causes, and Patagonia, known for its commitment to environmental sustainability, have cultivated loyal followings among values-driven consumers who seek to "vote with their dollars."

However, values-driven consumption has also led to increased scrutiny of corporate actions. Consumers are quick to call out companies that appear insincere or hypocritical in their activism, a phenomenon known as "woke-washing." When companies engage in activism without meaningful action or authenticity, consumers may respond negatively, accusing the brand of using social issues purely for marketing. This demand for authenticity places pressure on companies to back their statements with tangible actions to maintain consumer trust.

Boycotts and Brand Loyalty Along Ideological Lines

Corporate stances on social issues have resulted in both boycotts and heightened loyalty, with consumers aligning themselves with brands that reflect their beliefs and rejecting those that don't. For instance, brands perceived as woke may gain loyalty among progressive consumers but face boycotts from conservative groups. Conversely, companies that adopt traditionalist or patriotic messaging may attract support from America First advocates but alienate woke consumers.

This ideological loyalty has reshaped the competitive landscape, as consumers increasingly identify with brands on a personal level. Boycotts and counter-boycotts are common responses to corporate activism, as seen in cases like Chick-fil-A and Nike. Such polarization in consumer behavior highlights the growing importance of values in marketplace dynamics and underscores the challenges companies face in appealing to a broad audience.

Increased Demand for Corporate Transparency and Accountability

As consumers prioritize social responsibility, they are also demanding greater transparency from companies. Consumers want to know where products come from, how employees are treated, and what a brand's stance is on pressing issues. This expectation for transparency has led to a rise in "corporate accountability culture," where brands are held to higher standards and are expected to provide clear, actionable evidence of their commitments.

This demand for accountability has compelled companies to publicly disclose information on their operations, sourcing, and social impact. For example, fashion brands are increasingly expected to provide information on their supply chains and labor practices to satisfy consumers concerned with ethical production. While this transparency can build trust with values-driven consumers, it also exposes companies to greater scrutiny, making it crucial for brands to maintain consistency between their public statements and internal practices.

Broader Economic Implications of Corporate Activism

Corporate activism has had far-reaching effects on the broader economy, influencing investment trends, labor markets, and even regulatory landscapes. As companies incorporate social and political considerations into their business strategies, the economic consequences of corporate activism become more evident, affecting stakeholders beyond the direct consumer base.

Influence on Investment Trends: Rise of ESG Investing

Corporate activism has contributed to the growth of Environmental, Social, and Governance (ESG) investing, where investors seek companies that demonstrate a commitment to sustainability, ethical practices, and responsible governance. ESG investing has become a significant trend in the financial world, with more funds and institutional investors prioritizing socially responsible companies. This shift reflects the changing expectations of investors, who increasingly view social and environmental issues as material factors affecting long-term financial performance.

ESG investing has pressured corporations to adopt more responsible practices, as companies that fail to meet ESG criteria may struggle to attract capital. This trend has also led to the creation of sustainability-focused financial products, such as green bonds, which fund projects with environmental benefits. The rise of ESG investing demonstrates how corporate activism is shaping the economy by influencing investment flows and encouraging companies to prioritize social and environmental considerations.

Impact on the Labor Market: Demand for Values-Aligned Workplaces

Corporate activism has also influenced the labor market, as employees increasingly seek out values-aligned workplaces that reflect their personal beliefs. Many job seekers, especially Millennials and Generation Z, consider a company's social and environmental commitments when choosing employers. Companies that demonstrate strong commitments to diversity, sustainability, and social responsibility are often seen as more attractive workplaces.

This shift in employee expectations has led companies to incorporate social values into their workplace culture and employee policies. Brands with a reputation for corporate activism may attract top talent and foster a loyal workforce, but they may also face challenges in retaining employees if their values are perceived as performative or inconsistent. The demand for values-aligned workplaces reflects broader changes in the labor market, where corporate activism has become an important factor in talent acquisition and retention.

Regulatory Pressures and Compliance Costs

The rise of corporate activism has also spurred changes in regulatory landscapes, with governments increasingly implementing policies that encourage or mandate socially responsible practices. For example, new regulations may require companies to reduce carbon emissions, promote diversity, or disclose information on labor practices. These regulatory pressures reflect the growing influence of corporate activism on economic policy and compliance standards.

For companies, these regulations present both challenges and opportunities. While compliance with social and environmental standards can be costly, it also allows companies to gain a competitive advantage in markets that prioritize sustainable practices. Corporations that proactively address social and environmental issues are better positioned to navigate regulatory changes and build goodwill with consumers, investors, and policymakers. However, the added compliance costs and operational adjustments can impact profitability, particularly for companies that operate in industries with high environmental or social risks.

Corporate activism has transformed business practices, consumer behavior, and the broader economy, as companies increasingly align themselves with social, political, and environmental values. From adjusting internal policies to engaging in values-driven marketing, businesses are responding to the expectations of a more conscious and values-driven consumer base. This shift has fostered greater brand loyalty and consumer engagement, but it has also created challenges as companies navigate polarized public opinion and increased demands for accountability.

On a macroeconomic level, corporate activism has reshaped investment trends, with the rise of ESG investing encouraging companies to prioritize ethical and sustainable practices. In the labor market, employees are increasingly drawn to values-aligned workplaces, reflecting changing expectations around corporate responsibility. Additionally, regulatory pressures and compliance costs underscore the influence of corporate activism on economic policy.

As corporate America continues to evolve in response to social and political expectations, the impact of corporate activism will likely persist, shaping the future of business and the broader economy. While companies face risks in taking public stances on controversial issues, the alignment with consumer values has become an essential part of modern business strategy, reflecting the changing role of corporations in a society increasingly shaped by cultural and ideological divides.

Discussion on the Implications of Corporate Involvement in Political and Cultural Debates

As corporations increasingly engage in political and cultural debates, they are not only reshaping their brands and business practices but also altering the role of business in society. Corporate involvement in issues traditionally reserved for political and civic discourse has sparked discussions about the responsibilities, risks, and potential consequences of corporate activism. While some argue that businesses have a duty to address social and political issues, others contend that such involvement risks alienating consumers, undermining shareholder interests, and overstepping corporate bounds. This chapter delves into the multifaceted implications of corporate engagement in political and cultural debates, examining its effects on public trust, consumer relationships, employee morale, and democratic processes.

Erosion of Neutrality and the Redefinition of Corporate Roles

One of the most significant implications of corporate involvement in political and cultural debates is the erosion of neutrality in business. Traditionally, companies have focused on delivering quality products and services, refraining from taking stands on contentious issues to avoid alienating customers or stakeholders. However, as consumer expectations evolve and demand for corporate social responsibility grows, neutrality has become an increasingly untenable stance.

Pressure to Take a Stand

Consumers, employees, and advocacy groups now expect companies to speak out on issues ranging from racial justice and gender equality to climate change and immigration. Many believe that corporations, with their significant influence and resources, have a responsibility to contribute to societal progress. Brands like Nike, Ben & Jerry's, and Patagonia have embraced this shift, openly aligning with progressive values and publicly engaging in social justice causes.

However, the pressure to take a stand can backfire, as seen in cases where companies faced backlash for either supporting or failing to support a particular cause. For example, silence on high-profile issues is often interpreted as complicity, pushing brands into making statements they might otherwise have avoided. This pressure has redefined the role of corporations, transforming them from neutral entities focused on commerce to participants in cultural and political discourse. For companies, this shift brings both potential rewards, in terms of brand loyalty and consumer trust, and risks, including polarized responses and reduced flexibility.

Blurring the Line Between Commerce and Activism

The increasing entanglement of business with activism has blurred the lines between commerce and social advocacy. By aligning with specific political or cultural movements, companies risk being perceived as endorsing partisan agendas, which can complicate relationships with diverse consumer bases. For many critics, corporate involvement in social issues represents a concerning trend where businesses leverage societal concerns for profit, leading to accusations of "woke-washing" or shallow virtue signaling.

This blurring of roles creates ambiguity around corporate motives and raises questions about the authenticity of their engagement. When activism is perceived as a marketing strategy rather than a genuine commitment, it can erode public trust and reduce the effectiveness of corporate messaging. This is especially true for companies that espouse values without taking substantial action, as consumers increasingly expect transparency and accountability.

Consumer Division and Brand Loyalty Based on Ideological Alignment

Corporate involvement in political and cultural debates has reshaped consumer-brand relationships, creating new dynamics based on ideological alignment. In a polarized society, consumers often expect brands to reflect their values, leading to heightened loyalty for those that align with their beliefs and hostility toward those that don't.

The Rise of Ideological Consumerism

Corporate involvement in social issues has given rise to ideological consumerism, where individuals make purchasing decisions based on a brand's stance on specific issues. Consumers who support a brand's position are likely to become loyal customers, viewing their purchases as extensions of their personal values. For example, brands like Patagonia, which actively supports environmental causes, attract consumers who prioritize sustainability and ethical practices.

However, ideological consumerism also leads to boycotts and counter-boycotts, as individuals reject brands that conflict with their values. This polarization can limit a brand's reach, as companies that take explicit stances may attract certain demographics while alienating others. Companies must therefore weigh the benefits of loyalty from values-driven consumers against the risks of alienating those who disagree with their positions.

Brand as Identity

As consumers increasingly associate brands with specific ideologies, brand choices have become expressions of identity. For example, supporters of America First values may view brands that embrace traditional or patriotic messaging as reflections of their own beliefs, while woke consumers may gravitate toward brands that promote inclusivity and social justice. This shift from transactional relationships to value-based loyalty has made it more challenging for companies to maintain a broad, diverse customer base.

Brand identity rooted in social or political values can create powerful connections with consumers, but it also brings challenges, as brands risk becoming symbols of broader ideological divides. By aligning with particular issues, companies can inadvertently become targets in cultural conflicts, as seen in cases like Nike's Kaepernick campaign or Chick-fil-A's stance on LGBTQ rights. This evolution of brand identity underscores the complexities of corporate activism, as companies navigate the fine line between appealing to consumers' values and becoming mired in political controversies.

Impact on Employee Morale and Corporate Culture

Corporate involvement in social and political debates has significant implications for employee morale, recruitment, and retention. Employees increasingly expect their employers to reflect progressive values and address issues that align with their beliefs, leading to shifts in workplace culture and organizational priorities.

Employee Expectations for Values-Driven Leadership

Many employees, particularly Millennials and Generation Z, are drawn to companies that demonstrate a commitment to social responsibility. For these workers, corporate silence on issues like diversity, equity, and environmental sustainability can be a source of frustration, prompting them to seek employment with companies known for their activism. In response, companies have adopted policies and programs that reflect progressive values, from diversity initiatives to sustainability commitments, in an effort to attract and retain talent.

However, these expectations can also create challenges, as companies may face internal pressure to address issues they might prefer to avoid. If a company's values-driven messaging is perceived as inconsistent or performative, it can lead to disillusionment among employees. High-profile employee protests at companies like Google and Amazon, where workers demanded stronger stances on social and environmental issues, highlight the pressures businesses face in maintaining internal trust and engagement.

Corporate Culture and Cohesion

When companies take public stances on divisive issues, they may experience challenges to internal cohesion, as employees with differing beliefs may feel marginalized or alienated. For example, a company that aligns itself with progressive causes might unintentionally create an environment where conservative employees feel unwelcome or stifled in expressing their views.

This tension can impact team dynamics and overall productivity, as employees may become more focused on ideological differences than on collaborative work. Managing these challenges requires a delicate balance, as companies attempt to foster inclusive work environments while upholding their commitments to social responsibility. The impact of corporate activism on employee morale thus highlights the complexities of creating an inclusive corporate culture in a polarized society.

Potential Effects on Democratic Processes and Public Discourse

The involvement of corporations in political and cultural debates raises broader questions about the influence of business in democratic processes and public discourse. With their vast resources and reach, corporations have the power to shape public opinion and influence policy, potentially shifting the balance of power in ways that concern both consumers and policymakers.

Corporate Influence on Policy and Regulation

As corporations increasingly advocate for social and political causes, they are also more likely to engage in lobbying and political donations to advance these agendas. For example, companies supporting environmental initiatives may lobby for regulations on carbon emissions, while businesses promoting diversity and inclusion might support legislation on equal rights and non-discrimination.

While corporate advocacy can lead to positive changes in areas like environmental protection or human rights, it also raises concerns about the concentration of influence in the hands of a few powerful corporations. Critics argue that corporate involvement in politics risks prioritizing business interests over democratic principles, with decisions being influenced by companies rather than by elected representatives or grassroots movements. This growing influence raises ethical questions about the role of corporations in policy-making and the potential consequences for democratic processes.

Shaping Public Discourse and Polarization

Corporate activism has the potential to shape public discourse by amplifying certain issues and perspectives. When brands take strong stances on contentious topics, they contribute to the national conversation and can help bring attention to underrepresented issues. For example, corporate support for LGBTQ rights and racial justice has helped to normalize these conversations, creating a more inclusive public discourse.

However, corporate engagement in political debates can also deepen societal polarization, as consumers interpret corporate stances as endorsements of specific ideologies. When companies align with woke culture or America First values, they may contribute to echo chambers, where individuals are exposed primarily to perspectives that reinforce their own beliefs. This segmentation can reduce opportunities for cross-ideological engagement, further entrenching divisions within society.

The Role of Corporations in Civic Responsibility

As corporations continue to engage in political and cultural issues, they are increasingly viewed as quasi-civic institutions with responsibilities beyond profit-making. This shift has prompted debates about the appropriate scope of corporate influence, with some advocating for businesses to take a more active role in addressing societal challenges, while others argue that corporations should refrain from involvement in areas traditionally reserved for governments and civil society.

For many consumers, the expectation that companies engage in corporate social responsibility reflects a desire for positive change in a world where political gridlock often impedes progress. However, the growing role of corporations in civic life also raises concerns about accountability, as companies are not elected or directly answerable to the public. The tension between corporate influence and democratic governance underscores the need for a balanced approach to corporate activism, one that respects both the potential for positive impact and the risks of overreach.

Conclusion

The implications of corporate involvement in political and cultural debates are complex and multifaceted, affecting public trust, consumer behavior, employee morale, and democratic processes. As companies increasingly engage in issues that resonate with progressive or traditional values, they face both opportunities and challenges, balancing the potential benefits of brand loyalty and consumer trust with the risks of polarization and backlash.

The erosion of neutrality in business, the rise of ideological consumerism, the impact on corporate culture, and the potential influence on democratic processes all underscore the transformative role of corporate activism in modern society. While many consumers and employees expect companies to contribute positively to social issues, the growing involvement of corporations in political and cultural debates also raises important ethical and practical questions about the role of business in public life.

As corporate America continues to navigate this new terrain, the choices companies make will shape not only their brand identities but also the broader cultural landscape. The future of corporate activism will depend on businesses' ability to balance authenticity with responsibility, navigating the complex dynamics of a society increasingly defined by ideological divides and shifting expectations.

Chapter 6: The Policy Impact and Legacy of the Trump Era

Examination of the Tangible Policy Outcomes of Trump's Presidency in Areas Like Immigration, Trade, Foreign Relations, and Social Issues

The Trump presidency marked a period of substantial shifts in U.S. policy, reshaping the nation's approach to immigration, trade, foreign relations, and social issues. Guided by the "America First" doctrine, Trump's administration implemented policies that emphasized national sovereignty, economic protectionism, and a rejection of globalist principles, often resulting in stark departures from previous administrations. This chapter examines the tangible policy outcomes of Trump's presidency, exploring both their immediate impact and the lasting legacy these policies have left on the United States.

Immigration: Restrictive Policies and Border Security

Immigration was a central focus of Trump's America First agenda, with the administration implementing a series of restrictive policies aimed at tightening border security, reducing illegal immigration, and reshaping the legal immigration system.

The Border Wall and Increased Border Security

Trump's commitment to building a wall along the U.S.-Mexico border became one of the most visible symbols of his presidency. By the end of his term, over 450 miles of border barriers had been constructed, although much of this replaced or reinforced existing structures. The administration argued that the wall was necessary to secure the border, reduce illegal immigration, and prevent drug trafficking. While critics questioned the efficacy and moral implications of the wall, its construction symbolized Trump's prioritization of national sovereignty and security.

Beyond the physical wall, the Trump administration increased funding for border security, including additional surveillance technology, personnel, and immigration enforcement measures. These efforts contributed to a significant increase in deportations and arrests of undocumented immigrants, reinforcing Trump's message of zero tolerance for illegal immigration.

The "Remain in Mexico" Policy and Asylum Restrictions

Trump's administration also implemented the Migrant Protection Protocols, commonly known as the "Remain in Mexico" policy. This policy required asylum seekers to wait in Mexico while their claims were processed, a departure from previous practices that allowed applicants to remain in the U.S. during this time. The policy faced criticism from human rights advocates, who argued that it placed vulnerable individuals in dangerous conditions. However, Trump and his supporters contended that the policy was necessary to prevent fraudulent asylum claims and reduce strain on the immigration system.

In addition, the administration imposed stricter eligibility criteria for asylum seekers, making it more challenging for individuals from Central American countries to claim asylum based on gang violence or domestic abuse. These changes were part of a broader effort to reduce immigration and limit access to U.S. residency, reflecting Trump's stance on prioritizing American resources for American citizens.

The Travel Ban

Early in Trump's presidency, the administration issued an executive order that restricted travel from several predominantly

Muslim-majority countries, a policy that came to be known as the "Muslim Ban." Although it faced legal challenges, a revised version of the ban was ultimately upheld by the Supreme Court. Supporters argued that the policy was necessary for national security, while critics claimed it was discriminatory and fueled Islamophobia. The travel ban exemplified Trump's willingness to implement controversial policies in the name of security, underscoring the administration's prioritization of controlling entry into the country.

Trade: Economic Nationalism and Trade Wars

Economic nationalism was a hallmark of Trump's policy approach, with the administration pursuing protectionist trade policies aimed at reducing the U.S. trade deficit and bolstering domestic manufacturing.

Tariffs and the Trade War with China

Trump's trade policies were most prominently defined by his administration's trade war with China. Accusing China of unfair trade practices, intellectual property theft, and currency manipulation, Trump imposed tariffs on hundreds of billions of dollars' worth of Chinese goods. The tariffs sparked a series of retaliatory measures from China, resulting in a prolonged trade war that affected industries ranging from agriculture to technology.

The impact of the trade war was mixed. While the tariffs aimed to incentivize American companies to bring manufacturing back to the U.S., some industries struggled with higher costs and lost export markets. American farmers, in particular, were hit hard by China's retaliatory tariffs, prompting the Trump administration to introduce subsidies to mitigate the impact. The trade war underscored Trump's commitment to an "America First" economic strategy but also highlighted the complexities and unintended consequences of protectionist policies in a globalized economy.

Renegotiating NAFTA: The USMCA

One of Trump's key achievements in trade was the renegotiation of the North American Free Trade Agreement (NAFTA), which he frequently criticized as a "disaster" for American workers. The result was the United States-Mexico-Canada Agreement (USMCA), which included provisions aimed at protecting American manufacturing jobs, increasing labor standards, and improving market access for U.S. farmers.

While the USMCA was seen as a step forward by many of Trump's supporters, some economists noted that the agreement largely preserved the structure of NAFTA, with relatively modest changes. Nonetheless, the USMCA demonstrated Trump's determination to reshape trade agreements in favor of American interests, marking a shift toward bilateral and regional agreements over multilateral trade deals.

Tariffs on Allies and Trade Policy Shifts

Trump's trade policies also included tariffs on steel and aluminum imports from traditional allies, such as Canada, Mexico, and the European Union, which he justified on national security grounds. These tariffs strained relations with allied countries, as they retaliated with their own tariffs on American goods. Critics argued that these tariffs alienated key allies and disrupted global supply chains, while supporters believed they were necessary to protect American industries.

The use of tariffs as a negotiating tool became a central feature of Trump's economic policy, reflecting his belief that the U.S. had been disadvantaged in trade relationships. Trump's approach was a departure from the free-trade orientation of previous administrations, prioritizing American jobs and industries over maintaining close trade relations with allied nations.

Foreign Relations: Reorienting U.S. Global Priorities

Trump's foreign policy was marked by an emphasis on nationalism and skepticism toward traditional alliances and multilateral organizations. His administration reoriented U.S. foreign relations by focusing on bilateral agreements, reassessing alliances, and challenging international institutions.

Withdrawal from International Agreements

Trump's America First approach led to a series of withdrawals from major international agreements, including the Paris Climate Agreement, the Iran Nuclear Deal, and the Trans-Pacific Partnership (TPP). Each of these moves was intended to reassert U.S. sovereignty and independence from what Trump characterized as restrictive or unfair agreements.

The withdrawal from the Paris Climate Agreement symbolized Trump's skepticism toward global climate initiatives, as he argued that the accord placed undue burdens on the U.S. economy. Similarly, the decision to abandon the Iran Nuclear Deal was based on concerns that the agreement did not go far enough to prevent Iran from developing nuclear weapons. These withdrawals were celebrated by Trump's base as a reclamation of American autonomy but were criticized by international leaders and climate activists who argued that they weakened global cooperation.

Redefining Relations with NATO and Allies

Trump's presidency saw a reevaluation of longstanding alliances, particularly with NATO. He frequently criticized NATO members for failing to meet their defense spending commitments, accusing them of relying too heavily on the U.S. for military protection. Trump's calls for increased burden-sharing among NATO allies led to tensions within the alliance, with some European leaders questioning America's commitment to collective defense.

Despite these tensions, Trump's pressure on NATO members did result in some allies increasing their defense budgets. However, his approach also raised concerns about the future of the alliance and America's role in global security. Trump's stance on NATO exemplified his America First focus, prioritizing national interests over multilateral obligations, even within traditional alliances.

Engagement with Adversarial Nations

Trump's foreign policy also included unprecedented engagement with adversarial nations, particularly North Korea and Russia. His summits with North Korean leader Kim Jong-un marked a break from previous U.S. policy, with Trump hoping to negotiate denuclearization through direct diplomacy. While these efforts ultimately failed to achieve significant concessions, they reflected Trump's willingness to adopt unconventional approaches to foreign policy.

Trump's relationship with Russia was another area of contention, as critics argued that his administration's approach was overly conciliatory. While the administration imposed sanctions on Russia in response to election interference, Trump's personal interactions with Russian President Vladimir Putin sparked controversy and fueled suspicions of undue influence. These diplomatic engagements underscored Trump's focus on redefining U.S. foreign relations, sometimes at the expense of traditional norms and alliances.

Social Issues: Conservative Policy Shifts and Cultural Conflicts

On social issues, Trump's presidency represented a shift toward conservative policies that appealed to his base and challenged progressive gains in areas like LGBTQ rights, reproductive rights, and religious freedom.

Religious Freedom and Executive Orders

Trump's administration prioritized religious freedom, issuing executive orders that expanded the rights of religious organizations and individuals to express their beliefs. For example, Trump signed an executive order allowing religious groups to receive federal funding without adhering to certain anti-discrimination policies, a move welcomed by conservative religious organizations. His administration also supported exemptions for employers who objected to providing contraceptive coverage on religious grounds.

These policies were celebrated by America First supporters who valued religious freedom, but they faced criticism from progressive activists who argued that they eroded civil rights protections. Trump's emphasis on religious liberty reflected his administration's alignment with conservative values, appealing to evangelical and religious voters within his base.

Rolling Back LGBTQ Protections

Trump's administration took steps to roll back certain LGBTQ protections, including restrictions on transgender individuals serving in the military and the removal of federal guidance allowing transgender students to use bathrooms matching their gender identity. These policies were seen by supporters as necessary to protect traditional norms and maintain security within institutions like the military.

Critics argued that these policies represented a setback for LGBTQ rights, and activists protested the administration's actions as discriminatory. The rollback of LGBTQ protections reflected Trump's broader commitment to conservative values, emphasizing traditional gender roles and religious freedom over progressive social change.

Abortion and the Judiciary

Trump's appointments to the federal judiciary, including three Supreme Court justices, had a lasting impact on social policy, particularly on issues like abortion. With the confirmation of Justices Neil Gorsuch, Brett Kavanaugh, and Amy Coney Barrett, Trump created a conservative majority on the Supreme Court, which paved the way for potential changes to landmark decisions such as Roe v. Wade.

His judicial appointments were celebrated by conservatives who sought to restrict abortion rights and uphold traditional values. This legacy of judicial appointments is likely to shape U.S. social policy for decades, representing a significant victory for Trump's conservative base and underscoring the long-term impact of his administration on the country's legal landscape.

The policy outcomes of Trump's presidency in immigration, trade, foreign relations, and social issues reflect the tangible impact of his America First agenda. From restrictive immigration measures and protectionist trade policies to redefining alliances and shifting the judiciary, Trump's policies were designed to prioritize national sovereignty, economic independence, and traditional values. While these policies garnered strong support from his base, they also generated significant controversy and resistance, highlighting the deep ideological divides within American society.

As the nation moves forward, the legacy of Trump's policies will continue to influence public debate and shape the political landscape. His administration's approach to governance has left a lasting impact on U.S. policy and set a precedent for future leaders, illustrating both the potential and the challenges of implementing a populist, nationalist agenda in a diverse and complex society.

How These Policies Clashed with or Pushed Back Against the Prevailing Woke Narratives

The policies of the Trump administration directly clashed with or actively resisted the principles and values commonly associated with "woke" narratives. Trump's America First agenda, which prioritized national sovereignty, traditional values, and economic protectionism, stood in stark opposition to the progressive ideals of social justice, inclusivity, and global cooperation that characterize woke culture. In areas like immigration, trade, foreign relations, and social issues, Trump's policies were framed as a defense against what his administration and supporters viewed as overreach by progressive forces. This chapter examines how Trump's policies were both a response to and a rejection of the prevailing woke narratives, igniting significant cultural and ideological clashes across the country.

Immigration: Rejecting Open-Border Advocacy and Emphasizing National Sovereignty

Immigration policy under Trump became one of the most visible battlegrounds in the clash between America First priorities and woke ideals of inclusivity, globalism, and humanitarianism. Progressive narratives around immigration focus on open-border advocacy, compassion for asylum seekers, and support for immigrant rights, often positioning these as moral imperatives. Trump's administration, however, framed immigration as an issue of national security and economic protection, emphasizing the importance of controlled borders.

The Border Wall and Immigration Restrictions as Rejection of Open Borders

The construction of the U.S.-Mexico border wall and Trump's commitment to strict immigration enforcement symbolized a strong pushback against woke ideals of open borders and inclusivity for immigrants. The wall was positioned not only as a physical barrier but also as a symbolic stance against policies that Trump and his supporters viewed as encouraging unchecked immigration. By framing the wall as a defense against crime, drug trafficking, and economic strain, Trump's administration rejected the woke narrative that viewed immigration as a humanitarian right, emphasizing instead the importance of national sovereignty.

Progressive critics argued that the wall and accompanying immigration restrictions were racially motivated and disproportionately affected marginalized groups. In contrast, Trump's supporters viewed these policies as necessary to preserve American jobs, culture, and security, dismissing woke criticisms as idealistic and out of touch with the realities of illegal immigration's impact on American society.

The "Remain in Mexico" Policy and Asylum Limitations as a Challenge to Global Humanitarian Norms

Trump's "Remain in Mexico" policy and tightened asylum restrictions were responses to what his administration saw as the exploitation of asylum laws by economic migrants. Woke narratives champion asylum as a human right, emphasizing the need to protect vulnerable populations. Trump's policies, however, limited the ability of asylum seekers to enter the U.S. and remain during the adjudication process, aiming to deter what he called "fraudulent claims" that overburdened the immigration system.

This approach sparked outrage among woke activists and human rights organizations, who argued that these policies violated international humanitarian standards and placed vulnerable people in harm's way. Trump's administration framed the policies as necessary to protect the integrity of the asylum process and discourage exploitation of the system, directly challenging the woke perspective that prioritized compassionate, open-door policies for those in need.

Trade: Defying Globalist Economics with Nationalistic Protectionism

In trade policy, Trump's America First stance represented a clear rejection of globalist economic principles, which have long advocated for free trade, interdependence, and minimal barriers. Trump's approach challenged the woke narrative that prioritizes global economic cooperation, environmental responsibility, and ethical trade practices, instead emphasizing protectionism as a means of preserving American jobs and industries.

The Trade War with China as a Rejection of Global Economic Integration

Trump's trade war with China stood as a powerful rebuke to the progressive emphasis on global economic integration and interdependence. While woke narratives often view economic collaboration as a pathway to global stability and shared prosperity, Trump's administration argued that China's trade practices were exploitative, harmful to American workers, and a threat to U.S. sovereignty. By imposing tariffs on Chinese goods, Trump aimed to hold China accountable for what he saw as unfair trade practices, including intellectual property theft and currency manipulation.

Progressive critics argued that Trump's approach risked destabilizing the global economy and causing harm to both American and Chinese workers. In contrast, Trump's supporters saw the trade war as a necessary corrective to years of trade deficits and offshoring, framing the conflict as a defense of American industries against globalist pressures that, they argued, prioritized foreign interests over American jobs.

Tariffs on Allies and Renegotiation of NAFTA as Pushback Against Global Trade Norms

Trump's imposition of tariffs on goods from traditional allies and his renegotiation of NAFTA into the United States-Mexico-Canada Agreement (USMCA) also signaled a departure from woke narratives that advocate for global trade partnerships and multinational cooperation. The USMCA included provisions intended to protect American manufacturing jobs and increase labor standards, emphasizing Trump's belief that trade agreements should prioritize American interests over global considerations.

These moves were met with criticism from progressive groups who argued that Trump's trade policies undermined relationships with allied countries and were shortsighted in their economic impact. The administration, however, viewed these policies as a necessary shift away from trade deals that it argued had disproportionately benefited other nations at the expense of American workers, reinforcing the America First stance of self-reliance and economic independence.

Foreign Relations: Challenging Multilateralism and Internationalism

Trump's foreign policy stance further highlighted his administration's resistance to woke principles of multilateralism and international cooperation. While woke narratives often emphasize the importance of global unity and participation in international agreements, Trump's America First approach prioritized bilateral relationships, national sovereignty, and skepticism toward international institutions.

Withdrawal from the Paris Climate Agreement as Rejection of Environmental Internationalism

Trump's decision to withdraw the United States from the Paris Climate Agreement was a direct challenge to woke narratives surrounding environmental responsibility and collective action on climate change. The agreement, which is largely supported by woke activists, represents a global effort to reduce carbon emissions and mitigate climate change. Trump, however, argued that the agreement placed undue economic burdens on the U.S. and undermined American energy independence.

Critics accused Trump of prioritizing short-term economic gains over environmental responsibility and global leadership. The administration defended the move as a commitment to American jobs and energy production, framing the withdrawal as a defense against global environmental regulations that, in their view, disproportionately impacted the U.S. economy. This policy highlighted Trump's rejection of international commitments that he felt undermined American interests, clashing with the woke emphasis on environmental stewardship and global accountability.

Redefining NATO Commitments and Bilateral Relationships as a Rejection of Collective Security

Trump's push for NATO allies to increase their defense spending represented a pushback against the collective security model favored by woke narratives, which promote shared responsibility and multilateral cooperation. Trump's critiques of NATO echoed his America First ideology, arguing that the U.S. was shouldering an unfair financial burden in defending European nations. His approach encouraged a reallocation of responsibility among NATO allies, challenging the established norms of post-World War II international security.

This approach was viewed by woke advocates and many international leaders as undermining global stability and weakening alliances. Trump's supporters, however, saw his calls for NATO reform as a long-overdue correction that prioritized American security and financial interests over those of other countries. By redefining the U.S. role within NATO and other international bodies, Trump directly countered the globalist principles that woke narratives champion, focusing instead on strengthening America's independent position on the world stage.

Engagement with Adversarial Nations as an Unconventional Challenge to Diplomatic Norms

Trump's diplomatic outreach to traditionally adversarial nations, including North Korea and Russia, reflected a break from the conventional approaches supported by woke narratives of multilateralism and human rights advocacy. By engaging directly with leaders like Kim Jong-un, Trump sought to bypass traditional diplomatic channels, which are often grounded in collective security and long-term alliances. His administration's approach prioritized immediate goals, such as nuclear de-escalation with North Korea, over long-standing concerns about human rights.

This unconventional approach sparked significant controversy, with critics arguing that Trump's engagement undermined international norms and emboldened authoritarian leaders. His supporters, however, viewed these meetings as bold attempts to achieve peace and reduce conflict, contrasting with the woke narrative that emphasizes the need to uphold democratic values and human rights in foreign relations.

Social Issues: Resisting Progressive Cultural Shifts in Favor of Conservative Values

On social issues, Trump's policies often stood in direct opposition to woke ideals, prioritizing traditional family structures, religious freedom, and conservative cultural values over progressive advancements in gender and sexual identity, reproductive rights, and diversity initiatives.

Religious Freedom and Opposition to Certain LGBTQ Protections

Trump's administration championed religious freedom as a core value, often clashing with woke narratives that prioritize LGBTQ rights and gender equality. Through executive orders and policy changes, Trump expanded religious exemptions for businesses and organizations, allowing them to decline services that conflicted with their beliefs. For example, the administration's support for religious employers who objected to providing contraceptive coverage was framed as a defense of religious liberty against progressive policies that Trump's base viewed as infringing on individual freedoms.

Woke advocates criticized these policies as discriminatory and regressive, arguing that they compromised civil rights protections for marginalized groups. Trump's supporters, however, viewed these actions as essential to protecting religious expression and maintaining traditional values, directly countering woke narratives that prioritize inclusivity and gender diversity.

Appointments to the Judiciary and Opposition to Abortion Rights

Trump's judicial appointments, particularly to the Supreme Court, were a key element in his administration's pushback against woke social policies. With the confirmation of Justices Neil Gorsuch, Brett Kavanaugh, and Amy Coney Barrett, Trump established a conservative majority on the Supreme Court, creating a judicial environment that is more likely to revisit or overturn decisions such as Roe v. Wade.

This conservative shift in the judiciary alarmed woke advocates who viewed abortion rights as essential to gender equality and reproductive autonomy. Trump's supporters, however, celebrated the appointments as a triumph for conservative values, particularly among those who oppose abortion. By shifting the judiciary in favor of conservative principles, Trump's policies challenged the progressive social agenda and created lasting implications for U.S. legal precedent.

Rollbacks on Gender Identity Protections

The Trump administration's rollback of certain protections for transgender individuals, including restrictions on transgender individuals serving in the military, represented a direct challenge to woke narratives on gender identity. While progressive activists advocate for full recognition and protection of gender diversity, Trump's policies prioritized traditional gender norms and aimed to reduce what his administration saw as complications within military and educational institutions.

These rollbacks sparked significant backlash from woke advocates who argued that such policies were discriminatory. Trump's base, however, viewed these policies as essential to preserving the integrity and functionality of institutions like the military, rejecting the woke emphasis on gender inclusivity as excessive and misaligned with America's conservative values.

The policy clashes between Trump's America First agenda and prevailing woke narratives underscore the ideological divides that defined his presidency. From restrictive immigration policies to a reorientation of foreign relations, Trump's administration consistently pushed back against progressive ideals, favoring national sovereignty, traditional values, and economic protectionism over globalist and inclusive approaches. These policies not only reflected the priorities of Trump's base but also ignited cultural conflicts that continue to influence American society.

As the impact of these policies reverberates through subsequent administrations, the legacy of Trump's pushback against woke narratives will likely remain a contentious and defining feature of his presidency, shaping the political and cultural landscape of the United States for years to come.

Analysis of the Long-Term Effects of These Policies on the American Political Landscape and Global Relations

The Trump administration's policies, rooted in the America First agenda, have had significant and lasting effects on both the American political landscape and the country's global relations. By challenging existing norms, embracing nationalism, and redefining U.S. foreign policy, Trump's presidency shifted the dynamics of American governance and reshaped the nation's role on the world stage. As the immediate effects of his policies give way to broader, long-term implications, this chapter explores how Trump's legacy continues to influence U.S. politics, deepen ideological divides, and alter the course of international relations.

Reshaping the American Political Landscape: Polarization and the Rise of Populism

The America First doctrine introduced a populist ethos to American politics that mobilized a substantial base of conservative voters, transforming the Republican Party and reshaping the dynamics of political discourse in the United States.

Strengthening Populist and Nationalist Movements

Trump's presidency catalyzed a shift toward populism within the Republican Party, emphasizing national pride, economic protectionism, and a rejection of globalist policies. This populist approach resonated strongly with working-class Americans, rural communities, and others who felt overlooked by traditional political elites. Trump's policies, such as his trade war with China, immigration restrictions, and economic protectionism, reflected a commitment to these voters, whose concerns had previously been underrepresented in mainstream conservative politics.

This surge in populism has had a lasting impact on the GOP, as subsequent leaders have embraced America First rhetoric to appeal to this energized base. The Republican Party's identity has shifted as a result, with leaders prioritizing nationalism, skepticism of global institutions, and opposition to woke culture. This transformation suggests a long-term realignment within American conservatism, as Trump's populist legacy continues to shape the party's priorities and appeal to a base that expects its leaders to prioritize national interests above all else.

Intensifying Political Polarization

Trump's policies, often framed as a direct challenge to progressive ideals, contributed to increased polarization within American society. By adopting an openly confrontational approach to issues like immigration, trade, and social policy, Trump deepened divisions between conservatives and liberals. His administration's frequent clashes with woke culture, coupled with its resistance to the norms of political decorum, created a political climate in which compromise became increasingly difficult.

The legacy of this polarization is evident in the current political landscape, where ideological divides are deeper than ever, and bipartisanship has become rare. Trump's presidency established a precedent for unapologetically partisan governance, which has led to a new era in which both parties are less inclined to seek common ground. This intensification of polarization may have lasting consequences, as future administrations will face challenges in navigating a political environment that has become more divisive and less receptive to centrism.

Reshaping Public Perception of the Media and Institutions

Trump's rhetoric frequently criticized mainstream media and questioned the integrity of federal institutions, shaping public perception in ways that have endured beyond his presidency. By popularizing terms like "fake news" and accusing institutions of bias, Trump fostered a distrust of media outlets, the judiciary, and government agencies among his supporters. This skepticism toward mainstream media and institutions has influenced public attitudes, with many Americans now questioning the reliability of information and the impartiality of long-standing institutions.

The effects of this distrust are likely to persist, as skepticism toward established media and government has become deeply embedded in the American psyche. This distrust has significant implications for democracy, as it may hinder the ability of institutions to unify the public around shared facts or objectives, further complicating efforts to bridge ideological divides.

Shifts in U.S. Foreign Relations: The End of the Traditional Global Order

Trump's foreign policy marked a departure from the multilateralism that had defined U.S. relations with allies and adversaries alike for decades. The America First approach emphasized national sovereignty, renegotiation of alliances, and skepticism of international organizations, resulting in a shift in the global perception of the U.S. as a reliable partner.

Straining Relations with Traditional Allies

Trump's decision to impose tariffs on goods from traditional allies and his criticism of NATO's defense spending obligations created friction with long-standing U.S. partners. His administration's approach prioritized bilateral agreements over multilateral ones, and he frequently questioned the benefits of alliances that he perceived as unfairly burdensome for the U.S. This transactional view of alliances led to a cooling of relations with key allies, including members of the European Union and Canada, who grew concerned about America's commitment to shared defense and cooperative diplomacy.

The strain on these relationships may have long-term consequences, as allies reassess their reliance on U.S. leadership. Some European countries have already begun exploring avenues for greater independence in defense and trade policies, reducing their dependence on U.S. leadership. While efforts to restore these alliances have been made by subsequent administrations, the sense of mistrust fostered during the Trump era underscores a lasting shift in how America's allies view the reliability of U.S. support.

Reevaluation of America's Role in International Organizations

Trump's withdrawal from key international agreements, such as the Paris Climate Agreement and the Iran Nuclear Deal, signaled a rejection of the multilateralism that has long been a cornerstone of U.S. foreign policy. His administration's departure from these agreements was framed as a defense of U.S. sovereignty, arguing that global agreements placed undue restrictions on American policy.

This shift has had a lasting impact on international organizations, as countries and global bodies have been forced to adapt to the possibility of an unpredictable U.S. approach to multilateralism. America's retreat from international agreements has opened the door for other nations, particularly China, to assume greater leadership roles in organizations like the United Nations and the World Health Organization. While subsequent administrations may seek to re-engage with global institutions, the legacy of Trump's policies has signaled to the world that the U.S. may not always be committed to collective action, prompting a reevaluation of the global order.

Increased Tensions with China and Russia

Trump's policies toward China and Russia redefined America's approach to two of its most significant global competitors. The trade war with China introduced an era of economic confrontation, challenging the previous assumptions of economic interdependence and leading to a reconfiguration of supply chains and trade alliances. This shift continues to influence U.S.-China relations, as both countries compete for technological and economic dominance.

Trump's stance on Russia was more complex, as his administration imposed sanctions on Russia in response to election interference while Trump himself often appeared conciliatory toward Russian President Vladimir Putin. This dynamic created ambiguity around U.S.-Russia relations, but the emphasis on sanctions and military deterrence has persisted. Trump's policies underscored the importance of maintaining a strong stance against potential adversaries, a legacy that has informed subsequent U.S. strategies in confronting Russian aggression, as seen in the context of the Ukraine crisis.

Long-Term Impact on Economic Policy: Shifting the U.S. Stance on Trade and Industrial Policy

Trump's economic policies, characterized by protectionism and skepticism toward free trade, introduced a new approach to economic policy that has influenced the current thinking around trade and industrial strategy.

Normalization of Protectionist Policies

Trump's trade policies, particularly the imposition of tariffs and renegotiation of trade agreements, signaled a shift away from free trade and toward economic nationalism. His administration's approach normalized the use of tariffs as a tool to protect American industries and address trade imbalances, a departure from the pro-globalization stance that had defined U.S. trade policy for decades.

This shift toward protectionism has influenced subsequent economic policies, as both Republicans and Democrats have become more open to adopting protectionist measures in sectors like manufacturing, technology, and pharmaceuticals. The pandemic underscored the importance of domestic production, reinforcing the emphasis on economic independence that was a hallmark of Trump's agenda. As a result, the U.S. is likely to continue pursuing policies that prioritize domestic industry and reduce reliance on foreign supply chains, reflecting the lasting impact of Trump's America First economic philosophy.

Resurgence of Industrial Policy and Workforce Development

Trump's focus on revitalizing American manufacturing and protecting domestic jobs has contributed to a resurgence of interest in industrial policy and workforce development. His administration's policies, including tax cuts and deregulation, were intended to boost domestic production and create opportunities for American workers. While the outcomes were mixed, these policies prompted discussions on the need for strategic investments in critical industries, such as technology, energy, and infrastructure.

The emphasis on industrial policy has persisted, as subsequent administrations have also recognized the importance of investing in American industries to remain competitive globally. Policies that prioritize workforce development and support for skilled labor in key sectors have gained traction, reflecting Trump's legacy of economic nationalism and the focus on restoring American manufacturing capabilities.

The Cultural and Social Legacy: Redefining American Values and Identity

Trump's policies and rhetoric reshaped not only the political and economic landscape but also the cultural and social fabric of American society. His administration's stances on issues like immigration, religious freedom, and LGBTQ rights ignited cultural debates that continue to influence public discourse.

Redefining Patriotism and National Identity

Trump's America First agenda emphasized a form of patriotism rooted in nationalism, traditional values, and cultural heritage, resonating with segments of the American public that felt disconnected from progressive cultural shifts. His policies on immigration, trade, and national security reinforced this narrative, appealing to those who prioritized American sovereignty and cultural preservation.

This redefined sense of patriotism has left a lasting impact on American identity, particularly among conservative groups who view America First as a defense against what they perceive as the erosion of traditional values. This legacy continues to shape political discourse, as both sides grapple with differing visions of what it means to be American in an increasingly diverse and ideologically divided society.

The Influence on Social Policy and Judicial Precedent

Trump's judicial appointments, including three conservative Supreme Court justices, have set the stage for potential shifts in social policy on issues like abortion, LGBTQ rights, and religious freedom. The conservative tilt of the judiciary, solidified by Trump's appointments, has created a legacy that may shape American social policy for decades. Recent decisions and anticipated rulings on these issues reflect Trump's influence on the judicial system and the enduring impact of his administration's commitment to conservative values.

Woke Culture and Counter-Cultural Resistance

The Trump era ignited a cultural clash between progressive, or "woke," ideals and America First values. This ideological conflict, manifesting in debates over free speech, gender identity, and racial justice, continues to influence American society, as Trump's policies and rhetoric galvanized both supporters and critics. Trump's resistance to woke culture inspired a counter-movement that remains influential, with ongoing debates over cultural identity and the role of government in social issues.

This counter-cultural resistance to woke narratives has solidified a lasting legacy within conservative circles, who view the rejection of woke culture as a defense of free speech and traditional American values. As these cultural tensions persist, Trump's influence will likely continue to be felt in the public square, shaping the ideological battles that define American society.

The long-term effects of Trump's policies on the American political landscape and global relations are profound and multifaceted. By promoting America First principles and challenging existing norms, Trump redefined the GOP's identity, shifted U.S. foreign policy priorities, and influenced public perceptions of patriotism, economic protectionism, and social values. His presidency not only transformed American governance but also ignited cultural and ideological debates that continue to shape the nation's identity.

As the United States and the world adapt to these changes, the legacy of Trump's policies will continue to influence both domestic and international affairs, creating a lasting impact that will shape political discourse, policy decisions, and public values for years to come.

Reflections on the Successes, Failures, and Controversies that Defined Trump's Legacy in the Context of the Ongoing Cultural Conflict

Donald Trump's presidency left an indelible mark on the American political landscape, igniting intense cultural conflicts that continue to shape the national discourse. His policies, guided by the America First doctrine, redefined U.S. governance in key areas like immigration, trade, foreign policy, and social issues. As his administration confronted progressive or "woke" narratives, Trump's approach brought both notable successes and significant failures, sparking controversies that still resonate in American society. This chapter provides a comprehensive reflection on the successes, failures, and controversies that defined Trump's legacy, with particular emphasis on how his policies fueled and deepened the ongoing cultural conflict.

Successes: Reclaiming National Sovereignty and Strengthening the Conservative Agenda

Many of Trump's policy achievements align with his commitment to restoring national sovereignty, reinvigorating American industry, and promoting traditional values. These successes resonated deeply with his supporters, particularly those who felt alienated by progressive agendas and international agreements that, in their view, compromised American interests.

Revitalizing American Manufacturing and Economic Nationalism

Trump's trade policies, including tariffs on Chinese goods and the renegotiation of NAFTA into the United States-Mexico-Canada Agreement (USMCA), marked a significant shift toward economic nationalism. By focusing on policies that protected American manufacturing and reduced trade imbalances, Trump redefined economic policy to prioritize American workers and industries. These efforts were seen as a direct response to globalization, which his administration argued had eroded domestic industries and outsourced jobs. His policies earned him widespread support from working-class Americans who saw his approach as a defense of their livelihoods.

The success of these policies was evident in the rebirth of American steel and aluminum industries, as well as in sectors where domestic production was bolstered. While the long-term effectiveness of these strategies remains debated, Trump's administration set a precedent for future leaders to consider economic policies that prioritize national interests, a legacy that persists in ongoing discussions about American independence in global markets.

Shifting the Judicial Landscape

Trump's judicial appointments, particularly his three Supreme Court picks—Neil Gorsuch, Brett Kavanaugh, and Amy Coney Barrett—were among the most significant and lasting impacts of his presidency. These appointments solidified a conservative majority on the Court, positioning it to influence decisions on key social issues for generations. For conservative Americans, this was a monumental success, as it created a judiciary more aligned with traditional values, potentially reshaping rulings on issues like abortion, LGBTQ rights, and religious freedom.

By appointing over 200 federal judges, Trump's legacy extended far beyond his term, cementing a judicial framework that continues to reflect conservative principles. This success is viewed by many of his supporters as a fulfillment of his promise to restore what they saw as the country's moral compass, countering what they perceived as progressive overreach in the courts.

Strengthening Border Security and Immigration Reform

Trump's focus on border security and immigration reform was a defining aspect of his presidency. His administration's emphasis on constructing a U.S.-Mexico border wall, implementing the "Remain in Mexico" policy, and imposing travel bans on certain countries were all intended to curb illegal immigration and prioritize American sovereignty. These policies resonated with supporters who were concerned about the economic, social, and security implications of unchecked immigration.

While the efficacy and morality of these policies remain hotly debated, they underscored Trump's commitment to an America First agenda that prioritized national security and border control. The shift toward strict immigration enforcement reflected his promise to place American citizens' needs at the forefront, challenging progressive perspectives on open borders and inclusivity.

Failures: Economic Fallout and Alienation of Key Allies

While Trump achieved several policy goals, certain aspects of his presidency are widely viewed as failures, particularly in areas where his strategies backfired or had unintended consequences. These failures also reveal the limits and risks associated with his America First approach.

The Economic Consequences of the Trade War with China

Although Trump's trade war with China was intended to boost American industries and reduce the trade deficit, it also led to economic setbacks in various sectors. The imposition of tariffs resulted in retaliatory tariffs from China, significantly impacting American farmers, manufacturers, and exporters who relied on Chinese markets. To mitigate these effects, the Trump administration implemented costly subsidies for farmers, but the impact of the trade war on the agricultural sector remained severe.

Critics argue that the economic fallout of the trade war ultimately harmed American consumers and businesses, leading to higher prices and disrupted supply chains. While Trump's policies succeeded in challenging China's trade practices, the economic costs of these actions highlight a key failure in the administration's strategy. The long-term viability of trade protectionism remains contentious, as it has revealed the complexities and interdependencies of the global economy.

Strained Relations with Allies

Trump's America First approach often clashed with the expectations of traditional U.S. allies. His decision to impose tariffs on European goods, question NATO's purpose, and withdraw from international agreements like the Paris Climate Accord strained relationships with key allies in Europe and beyond. These actions were seen as a rejection of the multilateralism that has historically defined U.S. foreign policy, creating friction and uncertainty among allied nations.

The fallout from these strained relationships has had lasting implications, as some allies began reassessing their reliance on U.S. leadership. While Trump's policies aimed to prioritize American interests, they inadvertently weakened diplomatic ties and raised questions about America's commitment to collective security. These strained alliances underscore the limitations of Trump's foreign policy, as the cost of isolating traditional allies continues to shape global perceptions of U.S. reliability.

Policy Reversals and Challenges to Policy Longevity

Many of Trump's policy initiatives were met with fierce resistance and were swiftly reversed by subsequent administrations. For example, the Biden administration rejoined the Paris Climate

Agreement and reversed several of Trump's immigration policies. These swift policy reversals suggest that Trump's America First agenda, while impactful during his tenure, lacked the bipartisan support necessary for long-term sustainability.

The impermanence of Trump's policies reflects a broader limitation of his administration's approach. By pursuing highly partisan policies and rejecting opportunities for cross-party collaboration, Trump's initiatives became vulnerable to reversal, highlighting the importance of building broader consensus to ensure lasting policy impact. This failure to achieve enduring reforms illustrates the challenges of governing through unilateralism and the risks of policy instability in a polarized political landscape.

Controversies: The Cultural Conflict and the Polarization of American Society

The controversies surrounding Trump's presidency were fueled by his confrontational approach to governance and his willingness to challenge progressive ideals directly. His tenure was marked by a series of cultural clashes that intensified polarization within American society and reshaped public discourse.

The Rhetoric of Division and its Cultural Impact

Trump's rhetoric, particularly his use of inflammatory language to describe the media, immigrants, and political opponents, became a defining feature of his presidency. His frequent criticism of "fake news" and his labeling of critics as "enemies of the people" contributed to a polarized media environment, where mistrust and bias became more pronounced. For his supporters, Trump's unapologetic style was seen as a refreshing departure from political correctness, while critics argued that it eroded public trust in institutions and fueled division.

This confrontational approach to rhetoric has left a lasting cultural impact, as the divisive language of the Trump era continues to shape American political discourse. The cultural polarization intensified during his presidency, creating a divide in which both sides became more entrenched in their beliefs. Trump's rhetoric fueled a cultural conflict that transcends politics, as it has influenced how Americans view each other, the media, and the political process itself.

The Role of Social Media and Misinformation

Trump's presidency saw an unprecedented reliance on social media, particularly Twitter, as a means of communicating directly with the public. While this approach allowed Trump to bypass traditional media channels, it also sparked controversies related to misinformation, as critics argued that Trump's tweets often contained misleading or false information. His use of social media intensified the spread of polarizing narratives, as followers and detractors alike engaged with his posts, often reinforcing ideological echo chambers.

The controversies surrounding Trump's social media presence have had lasting implications for public discourse and media credibility. His reliance on platforms like Twitter to challenge traditional narratives and promote alternative viewpoints revealed the power of social media in shaping public opinion. However, it also highlighted the risks of misinformation, as his posts often sparked heated debates and furthered divisions within American society.

Controversial Policies on Immigration and Social Issues

Trump's stance on immigration, particularly his policies aimed at restricting asylum access and instituting travel bans, generated intense controversy. For many Americans, these policies were seen as an attack on inclusivity and compassion, while Trump's supporters viewed them as necessary for protecting American security and sovereignty. Similarly, his administration's rollback of certain LGBTQ protections and its emphasis on religious freedom clashed with progressive values, igniting cultural debates about civil rights and social justice.

These controversial policies underscored the deep ideological divide in the U.S., with Trump's policies often positioned as direct challenges to the woke values of inclusivity and diversity. His administration's approach to social issues contributed to a culture war that remains ongoing, as both supporters and critics continue to debate the boundaries of personal freedom, national security, and civil rights.

Trump's presidency will be remembered for its bold policies, divisive rhetoric, and profound impact on the American political and cultural landscape. His successes in reshaping the judiciary, strengthening border security, and advancing a nationalist economic agenda resonated deeply with his base, setting a lasting precedent for the Republican Party. However, his administration's failures, including the economic fallout of the trade war and strained relations with allies, underscore the limitations and risks of an America First approach.

The controversies that defined Trump's presidency reveal the depth of the cultural conflict that his policies and rhetoric exacerbated. From his confrontational approach to progressive values to his use of social media as a direct communication tool, Trump challenged the norms of presidential governance in ways that will continue to shape American society for years to come.

As the legacy of Trump's policies endures, his impact on the American political landscape and the ongoing cultural conflict remains a topic of intense debate. His presidency has set a new standard for how leaders engage with cultural divides, leaving a complex and multifaceted legacy that will influence future administrations and public discourse in America.

Chapter 7: After Trump: The Future of America First and Woke Politics

Exploration of the Current State of the America First Movement and Woke Politics After Trump's Presidency

With the end of Donald Trump's presidency, the cultural and ideological movements he influenced—America First and woke politics—have evolved, continuing to shape the American political landscape. While Trump's term amplified these two opposing narratives, they have taken on new forms in the years following his presidency. The America First movement, rooted in nationalism, economic protectionism, and traditional values, remains a powerful force within the conservative sphere. Meanwhile, woke politics, which emphasizes social justice, inclusivity, and systemic change, has solidified its presence within progressive circles, impacting policies and social norms. This chapter examines the state of these movements today, their influence on American society, and how they continue to reflect and deepen the nation's ideological divides.

The Evolution of the America First Movement: Redefining Nationalism and Conservatism

After Trump's departure from office, the America First movement has persisted as a central theme within the Republican Party, redefining conservatism and influencing policy discussions on national sovereignty, immigration, trade, and traditional values. Trump's influence on the movement remains strong, but new leaders have emerged, seeking to expand its appeal and adapt its principles to contemporary issues.

The Rise of America First Leaders and the Reinforcement of Conservative Identity

Although Trump no longer holds the presidency, his influence on the Republican Party endures through America First-aligned politicians who champion his vision. Figures like Florida Governor Ron DeSantis, Representatives Marjorie Taylor Greene and Matt Gaetz, and Senators Josh Hawley and Tom Cotton have embraced elements of the America First agenda. These leaders emphasize protecting American jobs, strengthening border security, and resisting progressive policies on social and cultural issues.

This new generation of conservative leaders has reinforced the America First identity, positioning themselves as defenders of traditional values and critics of globalist agendas. For many supporters, the America First movement represents a reclamation of American sovereignty and a rejection of perceived liberal overreach. By promoting these themes, America First leaders are reshaping conservatism to appeal to voters who feel alienated by progressive social changes and seek a return to what they perceive as authentic American values.

Immigration and National Security as Pillars of America First

Immigration and national security remain foundational issues for the America First movement. The push for strict immigration policies, including calls to finish the U.S.-Mexico border wall and enforce stronger border security, continues to resonate with conservative voters. For America First advocates, immigration represents a test of American sovereignty, with the border wall symbolizing a commitment to prioritize American citizens' safety and economic interests.

Additionally, national security concerns—often framed in terms of resisting foreign influence and protecting American jobs—have expanded to include issues like cybersecurity and technological independence. The movement's focus has evolved to address concerns about Chinese influence in American industries, intellectual property theft, and the need to maintain U.S. dominance in technology. These issues have solidified America First as a movement that emphasizes self-reliance and defends the nation against perceived foreign threats, in line with Trump's original vision.

Resurgence of Cultural Conservatism and Resistance to Woke Politics

America First leaders have increasingly focused on countering what they see as the influence of woke culture on American society. Cultural issues—ranging from debates over critical race theory and gender identity in schools to questions about free speech and religious freedom—have become central to the movement. Many America First advocates view woke politics as an attempt to rewrite American history, undermine traditional family values, and promote divisive ideologies.

This cultural clash has intensified since Trump's presidency, as America First politicians position themselves as defenders of conservative values and free speech. Policies banning critical race theory in schools, restricting transgender athletes' participation in sports, and protecting religious freedoms have gained traction within the movement. The America First agenda, therefore, continues to evolve as both a political and cultural force, challenging progressive norms and rallying support among those who feel alienated by rapid social changes.

The State of Woke Politics: From Grassroots Activism to Mainstream Influence

Woke politics has also grown and adapted since Trump left office, evolving from grassroots movements focused on racial justice, gender equality, and climate action into a more established part of mainstream progressive politics. The influence of woke ideals can be seen in policy initiatives, corporate practices, and cultural norms, reflecting a broader shift in American society toward greater awareness of social issues.

Woke Politics in Governance and Policy

Since Trump's departure, woke politics has found increasing influence within the Democratic Party and among progressive policymakers. The Biden administration has embraced elements of the woke agenda, such as addressing racial disparities, promoting LGBTQ+ rights, and advancing climate initiatives. Policies aimed at police reform, healthcare access, and environmental justice reflect a commitment to progressive ideals, with federal resources directed toward communities historically impacted by systemic inequalities.

At the state and local levels, progressive leaders have adopted woke policies as well. Cities and states across the country are implementing reforms related to criminal justice, housing, and education, often with a focus on equity and inclusivity. This influence has cemented woke politics as a significant force within progressive governance, with advocates arguing that these policies represent necessary steps toward a more just and equitable society.

Corporate America's Adoption of Woke Principles

Woke politics has also permeated corporate America, with many businesses adopting social responsibility and diversity, equity, and inclusion (DEI) programs. Corporations, particularly those in tech, finance, and retail, have embraced policies that promote gender and racial diversity, address climate change, and support progressive causes. This alignment with woke ideals has become a branding strategy, appealing to consumers who prioritize ethical practices and social responsibility in their purchasing decisions.

However, corporate adoption of woke principles has sparked criticism from America First advocates, who argue that these initiatives represent a form of corporate virtue signaling. Despite the controversy, woke culture's influence within the business world highlights its growing acceptance in mainstream society. As companies align with social justice movements, they contribute to the normalization of woke values, making them part of everyday corporate and cultural landscapes.

Influence on Education and Cultural Institutions

The influence of woke politics extends to educational institutions and cultural spaces, where discussions on race, gender, and identity have become increasingly prominent. Universities, schools, and cultural organizations have incorporated diversity initiatives, workshops on implicit bias, and curricula that explore systemic inequality and privilege. These shifts reflect the increasing mainstream acceptance of woke values and the commitment of educators and cultural leaders to address issues of social justice.

However, this influence has also prompted backlash from America First advocates, who argue that woke culture has overtaken educational institutions and limited free expression. Efforts to ban critical race theory and revise school curricula illustrate the pushback against woke principles, with critics contending that woke policies promote divisive ideologies. The clash between America First advocates and woke activists in these settings reflects a broader cultural conflict that remains unresolved, with both sides advocating for vastly different visions of American identity and values.

The Ongoing Cultural Conflict: America First and Woke Politics in Opposition

The America First movement and woke politics represent opposing worldviews, each with a distinct vision for America's future. As both movements continue to shape public discourse, their contrasting approaches highlight the cultural and ideological divides within American society, creating an environment of ongoing conflict and competition for influence.

The Clash over National Identity and Values

At the heart of the conflict between America First and woke politics is a fundamental disagreement over national identity. America First advocates view the United States as a nation defined by traditional values, patriotism, and self-reliance, prioritizing American sovereignty and historical continuity. They argue that woke politics undermines these values by promoting globalism, questioning historical narratives, and pushing for rapid cultural change.

In contrast, woke activists see American identity as evolving, defined by diversity, inclusivity, and the pursuit of social justice. For them, addressing historical injustices, systemic inequality, and environmental sustainability is essential to building a better nation. This divergence in values underpins the ideological conflict, as each movement seeks to assert its vision of what it means to be American in the modern world.

Media and Social Media as Catalysts of Polarization

Media and social media have amplified the tensions between America First and woke politics, creating echo chambers where individuals are exposed primarily to content that reinforces their beliefs. Conservative news outlets and social media influencers promote America First narratives, emphasizing traditional values and criticizing progressive policies. Meanwhile, mainstream and progressive media highlight social justice issues, promoting woke principles and challenging the America First agenda.

This media-driven polarization has fueled the ideological divide, as each side views the other with suspicion and hostility. The role of media in shaping these narratives has created an environment where ideological confrontation is heightened, complicating efforts to find common ground. Social media, in particular, has accelerated the spread of polarized viewpoints, with both America First and woke advocates using platforms to mobilize supporters and challenge opposing perspectives.

The Future of the Cultural Conflict

The cultural conflict between America First and woke politics shows no signs of abating, as both movements continue to wield significant influence over American society. Each side remains committed to its vision, with America First advocates pushing back against perceived woke overreach and woke activists demanding systemic change. This conflict is likely to shape future political battles, from debates over education and healthcare to discussions on immigration and climate policy.

As the cultural divide deepens, the potential for compromise becomes increasingly limited. The persistence of these opposing movements suggests that the United States may be entering an era defined by ideological segmentation, where communities, institutions, and even political parties align themselves along the lines of America First or woke ideals. The long-term implications of this divide will influence not only the direction of policy but also the broader narrative of American identity.

The America First movement and woke politics continue to define and reshape American society in the wake of Trump's presidency.

While America First advocates rally around traditional values, national sovereignty, and economic independence, woke activists push for inclusivity, social justice, and systemic reform. The ongoing clash between these movements reflects the deep cultural and ideological divides that define modern America.

As both sides continue to evolve and adapt, they shape policies, institutions, and public opinion, contributing to an environment of heightened polarization. The future of American politics and culture will likely be influenced by the continued competition between America First and woke narratives, as each movement seeks to assert its vision for the nation's future. This conflict underscores the complexities of an increasingly divided society, where contrasting visions of American identity and values fuel an ongoing battle for influence and ideological dominance.

Predictions on How These Ideologies Will Continue to Shape American Politics, Society, and Culture

As America moves beyond the Trump presidency, the enduring influence of the America First and woke movements is poised to continue shaping politics, society, and culture. These two ideologies, representing starkly different visions of America's identity and values, have deeply impacted public discourse and policy. As both movements evolve, they are likely to steer the nation in new directions, intensifying cultural divides and solidifying ideological factions. This chapter explores predictions on how these ideologies will impact future governance, societal norms, and cultural trends, and what this means for America's long-term trajectory.

Political Landscape: The Future of Partisan Divide and Ideological Alignment

Deepening Partisan Divide and Reduced Bipartisanship

The ideological rift between America First and woke politics will likely continue to deepen partisan divides, as each side emphasizes policies and rhetoric that alienate rather than unify. In a polarized environment, lawmakers may find it increasingly difficult to reach compromises or form coalitions that bridge the gap between these opposing views. As America First advocates resist progressive policies and woke activists push for systemic reforms, the possibility of meaningful bipartisan cooperation may diminish further, limiting Congress's ability to address complex, cross-cutting issues.

The persistence of these ideologies will likely harden party lines, with Republicans aligning more closely with America First principles—focusing on national sovereignty, traditional values, and economic protectionism—while Democrats embrace woke policies around social justice, inclusivity, and environmental responsibility. This division could entrench policy stagnation, as legislative progress is delayed or blocked by ideological disagreements, especially on issues like healthcare, immigration, and climate change.

Emergence of Ideologically Aligned Political Candidates

Both America First and woke movements have inspired a new generation of ideologically driven political candidates who are likely to run for office in the coming years. On the right, America First candidates will likely emphasize nationalism, border security, and traditional values, appealing to conservative voters who feel threatened by woke culture's perceived influence on American institutions. These candidates may take strong stances against immigration reform, foreign trade deals, and federal regulations, advocating instead for policies that reinforce American independence and protect American jobs.

On the left, woke-aligned candidates will likely continue to champion social justice causes, including racial equality, gender rights, and environmental protection. These candidates may advocate for policies such as criminal justice reform, universal healthcare, and green energy initiatives, seeking to address the systemic issues that are central to woke ideology. The rise of such candidates will cement the ideological identity of both parties, further polarizing American politics and shaping future campaigns around issues that resonate deeply with their respective bases.

Potential for Third-Party Movements

The sustained polarization fueled by America First and woke politics may create fertile ground for third-party movements. Voters who feel alienated by both extremes may seek alternatives, leading to the rise of centrist or hybrid political groups that aim to reconcile elements of both ideologies. These groups may promote balanced policies that address economic security, national sovereignty, and social equity without veering too far into either America First or woke territory.

However, the two-party system's dominance in the United States presents significant challenges for third-party movements, and the success of such efforts remains uncertain. Nevertheless, as polarization intensifies, the appetite for political alternatives may grow, especially among younger voters who are disillusioned with the gridlock and conflict between America First and woke-aligned representatives.

Societal Norms and Values: Redefining American Identity and Cultural Expectations

Clash over American Identity and Historical Narratives

One of the most profound impacts of these competing ideologies will be on the perception of American identity and history.

America First advocates emphasize a version of American identity grounded in patriotism, sovereignty, and traditional values, often invoking a narrative of American exceptionalism. Woke activists, conversely, call for a reexamination of America's history, advocating for an honest reckoning with past injustices related to race, gender, and class.

The clash between these perspectives may lead to an ongoing redefinition of national identity, with different regions, communities, and institutions adopting distinct interpretations of American history and values. Schools, for example, may face increased scrutiny and pressure to choose curricula that align with one of these ideologies. Monuments, holidays, and historical commemorations may become further battlegrounds in this debate over America's legacy, as each movement attempts to assert its vision of what it means to be American.

Evolution of Social Norms and Inclusivity in Public Spaces

Woke politics will likely continue to influence social norms around inclusivity and diversity, with public institutions, workplaces, and cultural spaces embracing practices that reflect a commitment to equality. Woke-driven initiatives such as diversity training, bias awareness, and gender-inclusive language will become more prominent in schools, corporations, and government institutions, as efforts to create inclusive environments are prioritized.

America First advocates, however, may push back against these changes, framing them as excessive or restrictive. In public debates over free speech and personal expression, the tension between inclusivity and individual freedom will remain a central issue, with each side asserting its values in areas like media, education, and corporate policy. The ongoing tug-of-war over social norms and inclusivity will likely shape public spaces, as both America First and woke movements advocate for their vision of how Americans should interact, communicate, and coexist.

Regional and Community-Based Cultural Differences

As these ideologies permeate American society, they may create stark cultural differences between regions and communities. Conservative areas are more likely to adopt America First principles, rejecting woke policies in favor of traditional social norms and local governance. In contrast, urban centers and progressive communities may embrace woke ideals, implementing policies that promote inclusivity, environmental sustainability, and social justice.

This regionalization of ideological adherence could lead to a more segmented society, where community values and local policies are heavily influenced by the prevailing political leanings of the area. The cultural impact of this segmentation may create enclaves of like-minded individuals, further reducing opportunities for cross-ideological engagement and reinforcing the idea that the United States is, in many ways, divided along ideological and geographical lines.

Cultural Influence: Media, Entertainment, and the Rise of Ideological Content

Ideological Polarization in Media and Entertainment

Media and entertainment are expected to become increasingly polarized as creators cater to audiences with distinct ideological preferences. Conservative media outlets and content creators will likely align with America First values, producing material that celebrates patriotism, self-reliance, and American heritage. Progressive media, on the other hand, will continue to advocate for social justice themes, focusing on stories that address inequality, diversity, and global cooperation.

As a result, viewers may gravitate toward media that reinforces their beliefs, deepening ideological echo chambers. Popular streaming platforms, news outlets, and social media influencers will play a significant role in amplifying these narratives, as content algorithms increasingly prioritize material that resonates with specific audiences. This ideological stratification within media will make it challenging for Americans to encounter diverse viewpoints, reinforcing the cultural divides that characterize modern society.

Rise of Ideologically Branded Products and Consumer Choices

The influence of America First and woke politics is also likely to extend to consumer behavior, as brands and products become associated with specific values. Many companies have already adopted woke-aligned practices, emphasizing corporate social responsibility, diversity, and environmental sustainability. In response, conservative consumers may increasingly seek out brands that reflect America First values, including companies that prioritize American-made products, conservative messaging, or rejection of woke policies.

This shift could create a marketplace where consumers make purchasing decisions based on ideological alignment, leading to the rise of ideologically branded products and services. As both sides prioritize values-based consumption, companies may be compelled to choose between aligning with woke or America First principles, adding a layer of political identity to brand loyalty.

Impact on Artistic and Cultural Expression

Artistic and cultural expression may also be shaped by the clash between these ideologies, as creators navigate the pressures of cultural expectation and audience demand. Woke politics, with its emphasis on representation, inclusivity, and social consciousness, will likely encourage artists to explore themes that highlight marginalized voices, historical injustices, and cultural diversity. This focus on socially aware art may lead to more inclusive storytelling in film, literature, and music, as creators aim to reflect contemporary social dynamics.

America First advocates, however, may push for art that reflects traditional values, patriotism, and American heritage. This may lead to the revival of conservative themes in cultural production, from literature that celebrates American history to films that emphasize family values. As artistic expression becomes increasingly ideologically charged, cultural conflicts may arise over the role of art in reflecting societal values, leading to debates over free speech, censorship, and the cultural role of art.

The lasting influence of the America First and woke movements will continue to shape the future of American politics, society, and culture. In politics, these ideologies are likely to deepen partisan divides, inspire ideologically driven candidates, and reinforce regional differences. In society, they will impact national identity, social norms, and the values reflected in communities and public spaces. In culture, they will polarize media, consumer choices, and artistic expression, as creators and consumers navigate the ideological expectations of their respective audiences.

As these ideologies evolve and adapt, they will contribute to an America where differing visions of identity, values, and progress shape not only political discourse but also everyday life. The ongoing influence of America First and woke politics will define how Americans perceive themselves, their country, and each other, underscoring the complexities of a divided society. Whether these movements will ultimately lead to greater understanding or further division remains an open question, as the ideological contest for America's future continues.

The ideological divide between the America First and woke movements represents one of the most significant cultural and political splits in modern American society. These competing worldviews, each with distinct beliefs about national identity, values, and progress, continue to influence nearly every aspect of American life, from politics to culture to public policy. As these ideologies evolve, there are several potential scenarios for how they might clash or, possibly, find resolutions in the future. This chapter explores potential outcomes, including scenarios of continued polarization, ideological compromise, and transformative shifts that could reshape American society.

Scenario 1: Escalation of Ideological Polarization and Social Segmentation

In this scenario, America First and woke politics remain deeply entrenched, with both movements intensifying their influence over different sectors of society. Rather than finding common ground, each ideology becomes more rigid, contributing to a more polarized and segmented American society.

Political and Regional Segmentation

America First and woke ideals could become the defining features of regional identities, leading to increased segmentation of the country along ideological lines. Conservative, America First values might dominate in rural areas and parts of the Midwest and South, while progressive, woke ideals continue to shape the culture of urban centers and coastal regions. This regional segmentation would affect local governance, education, business practices, and social norms, creating almost parallel societies with distinct values and priorities.

The political landscape under this scenario would see intensified partisanship, with state policies reflecting the dominant ideology of the region. States with strong America First influence may pass legislation that prioritizes traditional values, limits immigration, and restricts progressive social reforms, while woke-aligned states focus on policies related to social justice, environmental sustainability, and inclusivity. This split could lead to conflicting policies on issues like healthcare, education, and climate, creating further challenges for national unity.

Heightened Cultural Clashes in Media and Education

Cultural institutions—particularly media and education—would likely become more ideologically aligned, catering to either America First or woke perspectives. In media, conservative outlets may increasingly produce content that celebrates patriotism, self-reliance, and traditional family values, while progressive media champions diversity, inclusivity, and social justice. Educational systems would become focal points of ideological struggle, as school curricula reflect either traditional or progressive historical narratives, depending on the regional influence.

This ideological entrenchment would deepen cultural clashes, with each side viewing the other as a threat to American values. Media and educational content could become battlegrounds where ideological messages are explicitly promoted, reinforcing biases within each camp and making it difficult for individuals to encounter alternative viewpoints. Over time, this segmentation could lead to a society where ideological divides become permanent fixtures, reducing opportunities for constructive dialogue or common understanding.

Scenario 2: Compromise and the Emergence of Hybrid Ideologies

In this scenario, exhaustion from continuous ideological conflict leads to a push for compromise, resulting in the development of hybrid ideologies that borrow elements from both America First and woke politics. A shift toward moderation and pragmatism could help bridge the divide, especially if leaders from both sides seek solutions that address common concerns.

Political Leaders Adopting Pragmatic Policies

Faced with the limitations of partisan conflict, political leaders may adopt a more pragmatic approach, combining America First and woke ideals to address issues in ways that appeal to broader segments of the population. For example, an America First approach to economic independence could align with woke values of sustainable practices, resulting in bipartisan support for policies that promote domestic production of green technologies. Similarly, policies that enhance border security while creating pathways for legal immigration might appeal to conservatives while addressing progressive concerns around inclusivity and human rights.

This pragmatic blending of ideas could lead to a new political center that prioritizes problem-solving over ideological purity. As leaders adopt hybrid policies, they may succeed in fostering cooperation on issues like infrastructure, healthcare, and criminal justice reform, areas where there is potential for agreement on common goals. By finding middle ground, this scenario could reduce partisan divides and create an environment where solutions that address the needs of a diverse society become more achievable.

Evolving Cultural Norms Around Inclusivity and National Pride

In this compromise scenario, cultural norms around inclusivity and patriotism may also shift to reflect a balance between America First and woke ideals. A nuanced form of national pride could emerge, celebrating America's historical achievements while also recognizing the importance of inclusivity and social justice. This cultural shift would promote a more inclusive version of American identity, encouraging citizens to appreciate both the nation's traditions and its evolving diversity.

Schools, workplaces, and media would reflect this hybrid approach, teaching history with a balanced perspective that acknowledges past injustices while also celebrating progress. Companies might embrace both socially responsible practices and commitments to American-made products, blending consumer expectations for ethical practices with support for the national economy. Over time, this balanced approach could create a society that values both individual freedom and collective responsibility, reducing the intensity of ideological clashes.

Scenario 3: Transformation through Social Movements and Technological Disruption

In this transformative scenario, societal changes driven by social movements and technological advances reshape both America First and woke ideologies, leading to new forms of governance, social organization, and cultural expression. As technology continues to impact the way people live, work, and interact, the influence of both ideologies might be redefined, leading to unexpected alliances and priorities.

Social Movements Redefining the Scope of Each Ideology

Future social movements may blur the lines between America First and woke politics, challenging both ideologies to evolve in response to changing societal needs. For instance, a movement focused on economic justice and localism could appeal to both America First supporters, who value community self-reliance, and woke advocates, who prioritize equity and access. This convergence of interests could create new coalitions focused on issues like wealth distribution, housing affordability, and workforce empowerment.

As younger generations become more engaged in activism, they may bring fresh perspectives that transcend traditional ideological labels. For example, Generation Z activists might champion issues such as digital privacy, ethical AI, and climate resilience, appealing to concerns across ideological lines. These movements could inspire America First advocates to embrace certain social justice goals, while pushing woke activists to prioritize community and national interests in ways that are compatible with both ideologies.

Technological Disruption Shaping Governance and Social Norms

Advances in technology, such as artificial intelligence, blockchain, and renewable energy, could reshape both America First and woke ideologies by changing the way society operates. For example, AI-driven automation might create a new focus on workforce development and economic independence, aligning with America First goals of self-reliance. Simultaneously, the use of blockchain for transparent governance could appeal to woke advocates seeking equity and accountability in public institutions.

Technological innovations may also reduce the relevance of certain ideological disputes by offering new solutions to longstanding issues. For example, advances in education technology could democratize access to knowledge, making education more inclusive and addressing concerns about ideological bias in school curricula. Similarly, the adoption of renewable energy could reduce dependence on foreign oil, satisfying America First concerns about sovereignty while addressing the environmental goals of woke politics. This scenario envisions a society where technology mediates ideological conflict, creating new opportunities for collaboration and problem-solving.

Cultural Transformation Through Decentralized Media and Virtual Communities

Technological advancements in communication and media could lead to the creation of virtual communities and decentralized media networks that allow individuals to engage with diverse perspectives. In this environment, social media platforms might evolve to prioritize balanced content or use algorithms that reduce echo chambers, fostering more productive conversations and exposing individuals to a wider range of viewpoints.

These virtual communities could offer spaces for constructive dialogue, where America First and woke advocates engage in meaningful discussions without the pressures of public confrontation. By facilitating exposure to alternative viewpoints, decentralized media might help bridge ideological divides, promoting understanding and empathy between opposing camps. This cultural transformation could lead to a society where ideological clashes are tempered by opportunities for genuine dialogue and collaboration, reducing the intensity of polarization.

Scenario 4: National Crisis and Unified Response

In a scenario where the United States faces a significant national crisis, such as a major economic recession, environmental catastrophe, or external threat, America First and woke advocates might be compelled to set aside their ideological differences to address the urgent needs of the nation.

Rallying Around Shared Goals During a Crisis

In times of national crisis, ideological divisions often give way to a sense of collective responsibility. Under such circumstances, both America First and woke advocates may find common ground by rallying around shared goals, such as ensuring national security, preserving essential resources, and protecting the welfare of all Americans. This unity could inspire policies that draw from both ideologies, combining America First's emphasis on national strength and resilience with woke politics' commitment to protecting vulnerable communities and promoting equity.

For instance, in response to a severe economic downturn, leaders might adopt policies that prioritize job creation through sustainable manufacturing and local production, appealing to both America First values of economic independence and woke principles of environmental responsibility. A unified response to crisis could foster a renewed sense of national solidarity, demonstrating that America's greatest strengths lie in its capacity to adapt and work together when faced with adversity.

Strengthening National Identity Through Collective Effort

A crisis-driven response that combines elements of both ideologies could strengthen national identity, reinforcing the idea that Americans can overcome challenges by drawing on diverse perspectives and experiences. By focusing on a shared commitment to the well-being of all citizens, America First and woke supporters could contribute to a narrative of resilience, unity, and shared purpose.

This scenario might foster a more inclusive form of patriotism, one that celebrates both America's heritage and its capacity for progress. Through collective effort, Americans could find common ground in their dedication to the nation's future, creating a lasting legacy of unity that transcends ideological divides. Such a transformation could help heal the divisions between America

First and woke movements, providing a roadmap for navigating ideological differences while building a stronger, more cohesive society.

The potential outcomes for America First and woke politics range from continued clashes and regional segmentation to transformative compromises and unity in times of crisis. Whether these competing ideologies ultimately lead to greater polarization or new forms of collaboration will depend on societal, technological, and political developments, as well as the willingness of Americans to bridge divides in pursuit of shared goals.

Each scenario represents a possible future shaped by the ongoing influence of these movements, reflecting the complexities of a divided society. As the United States navigates these ideological currents, the interactions between America First and woke politics will continue to shape the nation's identity, values, and trajectory, highlighting the challenges and opportunities of a diverse and evolving society.

As the ideological legacy of Trump and the principles of woke politics continue to shape America, the role of new political leaders, emerging movements, and grassroots organizations will be crucial in determining how these influences evolve. With Trump no longer in office, his America First agenda has been embraced and redefined by a new generation of conservative leaders, while woke politics, driven by progressive values, continues to gain ground through a network of advocates, activists, and local organizations. This chapter explores the individuals and movements on both sides that are shaping the post-Trump era, either by carrying forward these ideologies or by transforming them to meet the needs of a changing society.

Emerging America First Leaders: Redefining Trump's Legacy and Expanding Conservative Populism

In the post-Trump era, several conservative leaders have stepped forward to champion the America First doctrine, each bringing their own interpretation of Trump's populist vision. These figures are not only preserving the legacy of Trump's policies but are also redefining them, adapting America First principles to address new challenges and appeal to a broader conservative base.

Ron DeSantis and the Rise of State-Level America First Policies

Florida Governor Ron DeSantis has emerged as one of the most prominent champions of America First principles, implementing policies that emphasize national sovereignty, individual freedom, and traditional values. DeSantis has taken a firm stance on issues such as immigration, border security, and restrictions on woke culture in education and public institutions, mirroring Trump's approach but with his own distinct style.

DeSantis's influence highlights the growing role of state-level leaders in carrying forward America First ideals. By promoting policies that align with the movement's focus on nationalism and cultural conservatism, DeSantis has demonstrated how America First can be applied within states, serving as a model for other governors who want to advance similar policies. His approach reflects an evolution of Trump's legacy, emphasizing pragmatic governance alongside a commitment to conservative values.

Senators Josh Hawley and Tom Cotton: Defenders of Economic Nationalism

Senators Josh Hawley of Missouri and Tom Cotton of Arkansas are key figures pushing forward the economic nationalism that is central to America First. Both have been vocal critics of free trade policies, which they argue have hurt American workers by outsourcing jobs and weakening U.S. industries. They advocate for stronger trade protections, anti-monopoly legislation, and efforts to reduce America's dependence on China in critical sectors.

Hawley and Cotton represent a shift toward a more economically focused America First platform, building on Trump's trade policies and expanding them into areas like technology, healthcare, and manufacturing. Their emphasis on protecting American jobs and industries resonates with working-class voters, broadening the movement's appeal beyond Trump's initial base. This evolution of economic nationalism suggests a future where America First leaders prioritize U.S. self-sufficiency and resilience in global markets, aiming to rebuild American industry as a bulwark against foreign competition.

Marjorie Taylor Greene and the Influence of Populist Activism in Congress

Representative Marjorie Taylor Greene embodies the populist activism that has become a hallmark of the America First movement. Known for her outspoken defense of conservative values, Greene has championed policies against immigration reform, LGBTQ+ rights expansions, and progressive education policies, aligning herself closely with Trump's original base. Greene's emphasis on direct communication with supporters through social media channels and public rallies echoes Trump's style, keeping America First sentiments alive among grassroots conservatives.

Greene's approach highlights the role of populist activism in advancing America First principles in Congress. Through vocal opposition to woke policies and alignment with conservative grassroots movements, she keeps the movement energized and influential. Her approach underscores the power of media-savvy representatives to rally public support and maintain America First's relevance in national politics, ensuring that Trump's legacy remains visible even outside the White House.

Progressive Leaders and the Institutionalization of Woke Politics

On the opposite end of the ideological spectrum, woke politics has been institutionalized through the efforts of progressive leaders, activists, and organizations committed to advancing social justice, inclusivity, and environmental sustainability. These figures are redefining woke ideals for a post-Trump era, focusing on embedding these principles within policy frameworks and public consciousness.

Alexandria Ocasio-Cortez and the Progressive Push for Systemic Change

Representative Alexandria Ocasio-Cortez (AOC) has become one of the most recognizable faces of woke politics within the

Democratic Party. Known for her advocacy on issues like climate change, healthcare reform, and racial justice, Ocasio-Cortez has championed legislation such as the Green New Deal, aiming to address environmental and social inequities through sweeping policy changes. Her unapologetic embrace of progressive ideals has inspired a new generation of activists and leaders who view woke politics as essential to achieving systemic change.

AOC's approach illustrates how woke politics is shifting from grassroots advocacy to mainstream political influence, with a focus on ambitious reforms aimed at reducing inequality and promoting social justice. By embedding these ideals within concrete policy proposals, Ocasio-Cortez is advancing woke politics as a legitimate political platform, pushing for changes that impact education, healthcare, the environment, and the economy. Her influence suggests that woke politics will continue to shape progressive agendas, prioritizing inclusivity and equity at every level of governance.

Senator Elizabeth Warren and Economic Justice

Senator Elizabeth Warren has become a key advocate for economic justice within woke politics, championing policies that address wealth inequality, corporate accountability, and consumer protection. Her proposals, such as wealth taxes on the ultra-rich and stricter regulations on large corporations, align with the woke emphasis on fairness and equity, seeking to level the playing field for marginalized communities.

Warren's focus on economic justice reflects an evolution of woke politics that goes beyond social and cultural issues to tackle economic disparities. Her efforts to regulate Wall Street and support workers resonate with those who view economic inequality as a structural barrier to social progress. By linking woke ideals to economic policies, Warren's work suggests that the future of woke politics will increasingly address wealth distribution and corporate influence, aiming to create a more balanced economy that prioritizes the needs of everyday Americans.

Grassroots Organizations and Community-Level Change

Beyond high-profile politicians, woke politics is driven by a network of grassroots organizations that work at the community level to address social injustices and promote equity. Groups like Black Lives Matter, the Sunrise Movement, and local justice coalitions have galvanized public support for issues ranging from police reform and climate justice to affordable housing and healthcare. These organizations amplify the voices of marginalized communities, using grassroots activism to pressure policymakers and influence public opinion.

The impact of these organizations underscores the role of community-based activism in sustaining woke politics. By mobilizing local communities, hosting protests, and raising awareness through social media, these groups are pushing for change from the ground up. Their efforts suggest that woke politics will continue to evolve through grassroots channels, as organizations adapt to the needs of their communities and advocate for policies that address local inequities. This decentralized approach ensures that woke ideals remain a dynamic force in American society, even as they face opposition from America First advocates.

The Role of New Movements and Hybrid Ideologies in Bridging Divides

As America First and woke politics dominate their respective sides of the political spectrum, new movements are emerging that aim to bridge these divides, creating hybrid ideologies that draw on elements from both camps. These movements seek pragmatic solutions to America's most pressing issues, focusing on unity and progress rather than partisanship.

Andrew Yang and the Forward Party: A Pragmatic Alternative

Former presidential candidate Andrew Yang has launched the Forward Party, an effort to create a centrist movement that addresses political polarization and encourages collaboration across ideological divides. By focusing on issues like universal basic income, democratic reform, and economic innovation, Yang's movement seeks to transcend the ideological clash between America First and woke politics, instead promoting policies that benefit all Americans.

The Forward Party's emphasis on pragmatic, solutions-oriented governance reflects a growing desire for alternatives to partisan gridlock. By appealing to voters who feel alienated by both extremes, Yang's movement represents a potential path forward for Americans who prioritize innovation, economic stability, and social progress without the divisiveness of traditional ideological labels. The success of this movement could inspire other leaders to pursue hybrid ideologies that prioritize unity over conflict.

Tech-Driven Movements for Decentralized Governance

Technology-driven movements advocating for decentralized governance and digital democracy are gaining traction among younger generations, who are increasingly disillusioned with traditional political structures. These movements promote concepts like blockchain-based voting, decentralized social media platforms, and digital currencies, aiming to create a more transparent, accountable, and participatory democracy.

The appeal of decentralized governance reflects a rejection of both America First's emphasis on traditional power structures and woke politics' reliance on institutional change. Instead, these movements advocate for a grassroots, community-driven approach that prioritizes individual empowerment. The rise of these tech-driven movements suggests that future political and social organization may be less reliant on traditional institutions, creating a new path for Americans to engage in governance that aligns with their values while avoiding entrenched ideological conflicts.

Community-Based Initiatives for Economic and Social Resilience

In response to the ideological clashes between America First and woke politics, many communities are forming local initiatives focused on economic resilience and social well-being. These initiatives, often organized by small businesses, non-profits, and local leaders, prioritize practical solutions to issues like affordable housing, local job creation, and environmental sustainability. By working outside the traditional ideological framework, these community-based initiatives foster a sense of unity and purpose that transcends partisan divides.

The success of these initiatives highlights the potential for grassroots solutions that address shared challenges, regardless of ideological affiliation. By emphasizing local self-reliance and collaboration, these movements could inspire a shift toward community-oriented governance, where citizens work together to solve problems in ways that respect diverse perspectives. This approach suggests a future where Americans focus on building resilient communities that reflect their values, rather than engaging in divisive ideological battles.

The future of America First and woke politics will be shaped not only by the influence of high-profile political leaders but also by the impact of emerging movements and grassroots organizations.

As new leaders redefine Trump's legacy and advance woke ideals, they are adapting these ideologies to address contemporary challenges and appeal to diverse audiences. Meanwhile, alternative movements focused on unity and local resilience offer a vision of governance that seeks to bridge ideological divides, creating a pragmatic path forward in a polarized society.

Whether through the influence of populist activists, progressive lawmakers, or centrist movements, the legacy of Trump and woke politics will continue to evolve, influencing America's political, social, and cultural trajectory. As leaders and communities shape these ideologies to meet the needs of a changing nation, the future of American identity and values will be defined by their ongoing efforts to reconcile differences, address shared challenges, and build a society that reflects the aspirations of all its citizens.

Chapter 8: Conclusions and Reflections

Summarizing the Key Themes and Findings of the Book

The Trump Revolt: Putting America First in a Woke World has explored the cultural and political landscape shaped by the collision between two opposing ideologies—America First and woke politics. These movements, each with its own vision for America's identity, values, and role in the world, have transformed the nation's social fabric, policy directions, and cultural dynamics. In this concluding chapter, we summarize the key themes and findings that have emerged through our exploration of these competing worldviews, their impact during Trump's presidency, and their continuing influence in the post-Trump era.

Theme 1: The Rise of America First and Woke Politics as Defining Forces in Modern America

One of the primary themes of this book is the emergence of America First and woke politics as defining forces that shape modern American life. America First, with its emphasis on nationalism, traditional values, and economic protectionism, has offered a rallying point for conservatives who feel alienated by globalization and rapid social change. Under Trump's leadership, America First transformed from a political slogan into a broader movement that continues to influence conservative politics and policies, particularly in areas like immigration, trade, and national security.

On the other hand, woke politics has emerged as a powerful progressive movement, focusing on social justice, inclusivity, and systemic change. Rooted in ideals of equity and accountability, woke politics addresses issues such as racial justice, gender equality, and environmental sustainability. By advocating for a reexamination of historical injustices and the promotion of diversity, woke politics has reshaped institutions, businesses, and communities across the country. Together, these movements represent competing visions for America's future, each with a distinct understanding of national identity, values, and progress.

Theme 2: The Cultural Clash and Intensified Polarization

Another central theme is the intense cultural clash that has emerged from the conflicting ideals of America First and woke politics. Trump's presidency amplified this divide, as his policies and rhetoric often directly challenged progressive values, while woke activists resisted and pushed back against the America First agenda. This ideological divide has created a polarized society where differences in values and beliefs have translated into heightened social and political tension.

Throughout the book, we explored how this clash manifests in various aspects of American life, including media, education, and public policy. The influence of these movements has led to regional segmentation and the alignment of individuals, institutions, and even corporations with one ideology or the other. The result is a society where political affiliations often dictate personal identity, friendships, and community dynamics, making it increasingly difficult to find common ground or engage in constructive dialogue. This polarization, driven by media amplification and social media echo chambers, suggests that the cultural conflict between America First and woke politics may continue to shape American society for the foreseeable future.

Theme 3: The Policy Impact and Legacy of Trump's America First Agenda

Trump's presidency and his America First agenda left a lasting legacy in areas like immigration, trade, foreign policy, and social issues. This book has examined these policy areas in detail, highlighting both the successes and controversies of Trump's approach. Key policies—such as stricter immigration measures, protectionist trade practices, and a reorientation of foreign relations toward bilateralism—embodied Trump's commitment to placing American interests above global commitments. These policies resonated with his base, offering a sense of reclaiming national pride and sovereignty that many supporters found deeply affirming.

However, these policies also ignited significant opposition from progressive and moderate voices, who argued that America First often conflicted with the values of inclusivity, international cooperation, and human rights. While some aspects of Trump's policies were reversed by subsequent administrations, his legacy endures in the Republican Party's ongoing emphasis on economic nationalism, immigration control, and skepticism of multilateral institutions. This enduring influence illustrates that Trump's America First agenda has left a complex, multifaceted legacy that will continue to impact U.S. policy debates.

Theme 4: Woke Politics and Its Institutionalization Across Sectors

Woke politics has expanded beyond grassroots movements and activism to become a significant force within institutional settings, including corporate America, education, and government. This book has explored how woke ideals around social justice, diversity, and environmental responsibility have influenced public policy and business practices. Many corporations now incorporate diversity, equity, and inclusion (DEI) programs and environmental, social, and governance (ESG) criteria as part of their operational strategies, aligning with progressive values to meet consumer and societal expectations.

The institutionalization of woke politics has not been without controversy, as conservative critics argue that these initiatives represent a departure from traditional values and prioritize ideology over merit or economic efficiency. Nevertheless, woke politics has established itself as a formidable influence, changing the way institutions approach issues of equality, representation, and accountability. This widespread adoption of woke ideals suggests that progressive values will continue to shape American culture, even as these practices face resistance from America First advocates.

Theme 5: The Role of New Leaders, Movements, and Grassroots Organizations in Shaping the Future

As America enters the post-Trump era, the legacy of America First and woke politics is carried forward by new leaders, emerging movements, and grassroots organizations that adapt these ideologies to address contemporary issues. From conservative leaders like Ron DeSantis and Josh Hawley to progressive voices like Alexandria Ocasio-Cortez and grassroots organizations, each plays a role in shaping the trajectory of these movements.

These leaders and organizations have adapted the principles of America First and woke politics, ensuring that these ideologies evolve to meet new challenges. For instance, America First leaders are expanding the movement to address economic independence and technological innovation, while woke advocates focus on climate justice, racial equity, and economic reform. The ongoing efforts of these leaders suggest that the influence of both ideologies will remain strong, with new forms of advocacy and policy shaping the landscape of American politics.

Theme 6: Possible Paths Forward and Potential Resolutions

The final theme of this book considers potential paths forward for resolving or managing the conflict between America First and woke politics. While the divide between these ideologies is deep, several scenarios offer the possibility of compromise, adaptation, or transformation. Pragmatic leaders and emerging hybrid movements may attempt to blend elements of both ideologies, addressing shared concerns like economic stability, local resilience, and community well-being.

Alternatively, social movements focused on grassroots solutions and decentralized governance could offer a new way to address issues that have divided the nation. In the face of a significant national crisis, such as an economic recession or environmental disaster, America First and woke advocates might be compelled to unite in pursuit of shared goals. These scenarios highlight the potential for Americans to bridge divides and find common ground, though the road to unity remains uncertain.

In The Trump Revolt: Putting America First in a Woke World, we have examined the cultural and political forces that define the current era, exploring the legacies of Trump's America First agenda and the growing influence of woke politics. The key themes and findings presented in this book underscore the complexity of America's ideological landscape, where opposing values and visions for the future fuel ongoing cultural clashes and policy debates.

As these movements continue to shape America, the future of national unity, governance, and cultural identity will depend on the willingness of leaders, institutions, and citizens to navigate these divides. Whether through continued conflict, pragmatic compromise, or transformative social movements, America will confront the challenge of defining its identity and values in a world shaped by these two powerful ideologies. The ongoing evolution of America First and woke politics will undoubtedly impact the nation's journey, guiding it toward a future that reflects the diverse aspirations and convictions of its people.

Offering Reflections on the Significance of the Trump Revolt in the Context of the Cultural and Ideological Shifts in America

The Trump presidency marked a profound shift in American politics and culture, a "revolt" that reshaped the nation's ideological landscape and brought underlying cultural tensions to the forefront. The "Trump revolt" was more than a political movement; it represented a powerful wave of populist energy, a forceful response to the rapid social and economic changes that have left millions of Americans feeling unheard, disenfranchised, and alienated. This chapter reflects on the lasting significance of this revolt, examining how it has influenced the way Americans view themselves, their country, and their values within the context of an ever-evolving cultural and ideological landscape.

Reclaiming a Voice: Populism and the Power of the Forgotten

At its core, the Trump revolt was a populist uprising that resonated with individuals who felt marginalized by globalism, urbanization, and the dominance of elite institutions. These citizens, often from rural areas or manufacturing towns, saw Trump as a leader who understood their frustrations and promised to restore their place in American society. For them, "America First" was not just a policy slogan but a call to reclaim pride, autonomy, and the dignity that they felt had been eroded by an increasingly globalized world.

Trump's rhetoric of reclaiming the forgotten America gave these individuals a voice, positioning them as essential players in the nation's future rather than relics of its past. The revolt was significant because it demonstrated the potency of grassroots power and the discontent brewing within American communities that felt ignored by mainstream political discourse. This populist resurgence reasserted the importance of domestic priorities, national sovereignty, and economic independence—issues that had been sidelined by decades of bipartisan support for globalization.

Reshaping Conservatism and Redefining American Nationalism

The Trump revolt redefined American conservatism, steering it away from traditional Republican ideals centered on free-market capitalism and limited government intervention. Instead, Trump's approach blended nationalism, economic protectionism, and cultural conservatism, creating a new blueprint for American identity rooted in a shared sense of patriotism, tradition, and skepticism toward external influences. This reimagined version of conservatism resonated deeply with Trump's supporters, who saw in it a reaffirmation of their values and a defense against progressive social shifts they felt had left their beliefs under siege.

By promoting an "America First" agenda, Trump tapped into an enduring form of nationalism that celebrated American uniqueness and prioritized the needs of American citizens over foreign commitments. This shift toward a more insular, self-reliant vision of national identity marked a significant ideological departure, contrasting sharply with the inclusive, globalist ideals that have come to define woke politics. Trump's version of American nationalism, centered on sovereignty and self-preservation, continues to shape conservative thought and influence the broader cultural debate over what it means to be American.

The Cultural Clash and the Heightening of Ideological Divides

The Trump revolt ignited a cultural clash that has since deepened the ideological divide in America, pitting traditionalist values against progressive ideals. This division is not merely political but profoundly cultural, touching on identity, morality, and the role of the United States in the world. While Trump's America First movement emphasized traditional values, patriotism, and a sense of American exceptionalism, woke politics championed social justice, diversity, and a call to confront systemic inequalities.

The significance of this ideological divide lies in its intensity and pervasiveness. For many Americans, these competing ideologies are not just political positions but reflections of their core values and sense of self. This has created an "us versus them" mentality, where each side views the other as not only different but fundamentally opposed to their way of life. This cultural divide has reshaped social relationships, community dynamics, and even consumer behavior, as individuals increasingly align their choices with their ideological beliefs. The Trump revolt underscored and accelerated these divides, revealing the challenges of fostering unity in a country increasingly segmented by contrasting worldviews.

Disrupting Political Norms and Challenging Institutional Power

Trump's presidency disrupted longstanding political norms, challenging the authority and credibility of traditional institutions, including the media, academia, and even the political establishment itself. His willingness to confront and question these institutions resonated with supporters who felt that America's elite had become out of touch, prioritizing their own interests over those of the average citizen. By criticizing "fake news" and denouncing entrenched elites, Trump challenged the power structures that many Americans believed had monopolized political discourse.

The significance of this disruption extends beyond Trump's presidency, as Americans continue to question the role and legitimacy of traditional institutions. This distrust has led to a rise in alternative media, grassroots organizations, and decentralized political movements that bypass mainstream channels. The Trump revolt thus highlighted a growing skepticism toward centralized authority, reflecting a shift in American society toward greater self-reliance, personal responsibility, and local engagement. This questioning of institutional power has set a precedent that will likely influence future political discourse, pushing leaders to address the grievances of citizens who feel disconnected from elite institutions.

Reinforcing the Push for Social Justice and Woke Ideals

Ironically, the Trump revolt also played a significant role in energizing the progressive push for social justice and woke politics. In response to Trump's policies and rhetoric, which many viewed as regressive or exclusionary, progressive activists mobilized to advocate for diversity, inclusion, and systemic change. Woke politics, which emphasizes equity, representation, and social consciousness, gained momentum as a counter-movement to America First ideals, expanding from activism into mainstream institutions, corporations, and local governments.

This polarization had a reinforcing effect, as both sides became more entrenched in their positions. Trump's revolt catalyzed woke politics, inspiring many progressives to rally behind causes like racial justice, environmental sustainability, and gender equality. The significance of this response lies in its institutionalization; woke ideals have now become central to progressive policy platforms, business practices, and educational agendas. This dynamic, where each movement energizes the other, suggests that the cultural and ideological shifts initiated by Trump's revolt will continue to shape American society, as both America First and woke politics influence the norms, values, and policies of future generations.

The Enduring Legacy of Trump's Revolt: A Reframing of American Politics

Perhaps the most enduring significance of the Trump revolt is its reframing of American politics as a contest between populist nationalism and progressive social justice. Trump's presidency highlighted that the traditional left-right divide no longer captures the complexities of American society, where cultural values, identity, and ideology play as significant a role as policy preferences. The emergence of America First and woke politics as dominant forces reflects a realignment of American political discourse, where the questions of national identity, cultural values, and America's place in the world are at the forefront.

This reframing has also expanded the political spectrum, giving rise to leaders and movements that do not fit neatly within traditional party lines. As future leaders navigate the legacies of America First and woke politics, they will face the challenge of addressing the cultural divides exposed by Trump's revolt, balancing the demands of a population that is increasingly divided along ideological and cultural lines. This shift represents a profound change in the way Americans view politics, signaling a move toward values-driven discourse where social and cultural issues take precedence over economic or foreign policy.

The Trump revolt was a defining moment in American history, a populist uprising that reasserted traditional values, challenged progressive ideals, and disrupted the political establishment. Its significance lies not only in the policies enacted during Trump's presidency but in the cultural and ideological shifts it ignited, shifts that continue to shape American society in profound ways. As the nation moves forward, the legacies of America First and woke politics will remain influential, reflecting an America that is grappling with its identity, values, and place in a rapidly changing world.

This revolt has set the stage for an era of intense ideological contestation, where questions of nationalism, social justice, and cultural values dominate the public discourse. The Trump revolt has forever changed the landscape of American politics, sparking a debate over what it means to be American, a debate that will continue to evolve as future generations navigate the complexities of a diverse and divided society. Through its impact on ideology, identity, and institutions, the Trump revolt will remain a powerful influence, reminding Americans of the enduring power of cultural and ideological movements to shape the nation's course.

A Call for Dialogue, Understanding, and Potential Pathways Toward Bridging the Divide Between the America First and Woke Movements

As America stands at a crossroads shaped by the intense ideological clash between America First and woke movements, it faces an urgent question: Can Americans bridge this divide and find a way forward together? The deep polarization that characterizes today's social and political landscape has significant implications for national unity, governance, and the health of democracy itself. If America is to thrive as a diverse and democratic society, it must confront these divides with empathy, openness, and a willingness to engage in genuine dialogue. This chapter calls for a renewed commitment to understanding and presents pathways for bridging the ideological rift, emphasizing that unity does not require uniformity but a shared commitment to respectful coexistence and constructive debate.

Embracing Dialogue Over Demonization

In a society where media and political rhetoric often amplify divisions, fostering dialogue over demonization is crucial for breaking down ideological walls. Both America First and woke advocates often view the opposing side as an existential threat to their values and way of life, creating a dynamic where debate becomes combat, and opponents are treated as enemies. Reframing the conversation is essential to creating spaces where people can discuss their differences without fear of condemnation or ridicule.

Promoting Open Forums for Civil Discourse

One approach to fostering dialogue is creating more open forums for civil discourse, where individuals can discuss difficult topics in a structured and respectful environment. Town halls, community centers, and even online platforms can serve as spaces for individuals to share their perspectives, listen to others, and engage in constructive conversation. Such forums should be guided by principles of respect and open-mindedness, encouraging participants to focus on understanding rather than winning an argument.

Encouraging Leaders to Model Respectful Dialogue

Political and community leaders have a unique responsibility to model respectful dialogue and discourage rhetoric that vilifies opposing viewpoints. When leaders prioritize respectful engagement, they set a tone that can help to de-escalate tensions and create an environment more conducive to understanding. Leaders from both America First and woke movements who engage in civil dialogue can serve as examples of how individuals can stand by their principles while still recognizing the humanity of those who disagree with them.

Prioritizing Media Literacy and Responsible Consumption

Media plays a powerful role in shaping public perceptions of opposing ideologies. Encouraging media literacy can help individuals approach news and social media with a critical eye, reducing the impact of sensationalized or biased content. When people are better equipped to analyze media sources and question inflammatory narratives, they are more likely to approach political discussions with a balanced perspective, making meaningful dialogue more attainable.

Building Empathy and Humanizing Opposing Views

Empathy is foundational to bridging divides, as it enables individuals to see beyond labels and recognize the personal experiences and values that shape others' beliefs. Both America First and woke advocates often hold their beliefs as deeply personal, grounded in specific lived experiences, fears, and hopes for the future. Cultivating empathy allows individuals to move past stereotypes and gain a deeper understanding of why others hold the views they do.

Highlighting Personal Stories and Shared Struggles

One effective way to foster empathy is by sharing personal stories that highlight the challenges and aspirations common to all Americans. Both America First supporters and woke advocates are driven by desires for security, opportunity, justice, and respect, even if they differ in how they believe these goals should be achieved. By focusing on personal stories that humanize each side, individuals may find it easier to empathize with perspectives they once viewed as alien or antagonistic.

Encouraging Cross-Cultural and Ideological Exchanges

Programs that encourage exchanges between communities with differing ideological leanings can be powerful tools for building empathy. For example, community exchange programs or discussion groups that bring together people from rural and urban areas, different ethnic backgrounds, or varying socioeconomic levels can expose participants to new perspectives. Such exchanges enable individuals to learn about the values, concerns, and experiences that shape each other's beliefs, helping to dissolve misconceptions and stereotypes.

Educational Initiatives That Teach Empathy and Perspective-Taking

Integrating empathy-focused initiatives in education can help young Americans develop the skills needed to navigate ideological diversity. Curricula that include discussions on perspective-taking, active listening, and conflict resolution equip students with the tools to engage in respectful dialogue. By instilling these values from a young age, educators can create a foundation for future generations who are more adept at bridging divides and embracing ideological diversity.

Finding Common Ground Through Shared Values and Goals

Despite their differences, both America First and woke movements are driven by a desire to improve America, even if their visions for that improvement differ. Recognizing shared values and goals can create pathways for cooperation, as individuals work together on issues that transcend ideological divides. By identifying areas where there is mutual interest, America First and woke advocates can collaborate on initiatives that benefit all Americans.

Focusing on Local Initiatives and Community Building

Many Americans, regardless of ideological affiliation, care deeply about their communities and want to see them thrive. Local initiatives focused on improving infrastructure, public safety, education, and economic opportunities can create opportunities for individuals to collaborate across divides. Working together on tangible projects fosters a sense of shared purpose and helps to build relationships that transcend political differences.

Addressing Economic Inequality and Workforce Development

Economic security is a priority for both America First and woke advocates, though they may approach it differently. Collaborative efforts to address economic inequality, create jobs, and provide workforce development programs can offer common ground. By working together on initiatives that promote fair wages, job training, and economic resilience, both movements can contribute to an economy that benefits all Americans, reducing the financial anxieties that often fuel ideological divides.

Promoting Civic Education and Participation

Civic engagement and an informed citizenry are essential for a healthy democracy. America First and woke advocates can unite in support of programs that promote civic education, encourage voting, and strengthen democratic institutions. By investing in civic participation, individuals from both movements affirm their commitment to a democratic process where all voices are heard and respected. Strengthening democratic engagement can also create an environment where ideological differences are managed constructively rather than divisively.

Embracing a Pluralistic Society: Unity Without Uniformity

America's strength has long been rooted in its diversity, a tapestry of cultural, ideological, and personal backgrounds woven together by a commitment to shared democratic principles. Embracing this diversity requires acknowledging that unity does not mean uniformity; Americans do not have to agree on every issue to coexist respectfully. By fostering a spirit of pluralism—where differing beliefs and values can coexist—America can find a way to move forward without requiring conformity.

Recognizing the Value of Ideological Diversity

Both America First and woke movements contribute valuable perspectives that enrich American society. America First's emphasis on national pride, cultural heritage, and community resilience balances woke ideals of social justice, inclusivity, and equity. Embracing ideological diversity means recognizing that both sides have insights to offer and that America is stronger when it draws from a range of perspectives. By valuing ideological diversity, Americans can create a society that respects differing views and finds strength in pluralism.

Promoting Policies That Protect Freedom of Expression and Belief

A pluralistic society depends on protecting freedom of expression, ensuring that individuals can voice their beliefs without fear of censorship or reprisal. Policies that uphold these freedoms enable individuals from both America First and woke movements to express themselves, engage in debates, and challenge each other constructively. Protecting these freedoms affirms America's commitment to democratic principles and provides a foundation for peaceful coexistence in a diverse society.

Encouraging a Culture of Mutual Respect and Collaboration

Ultimately, bridging the divide between America First and woke movements requires cultivating a culture of mutual respect. When individuals approach differences with curiosity and an openness to learning, they create a foundation for collaborative problem-solving. This culture of respect can be built in families, schools, workplaces, and communities, creating spaces where Americans can engage with one another's perspectives, work through disagreements, and find common solutions.

The ideological rift between America First and woke movements is emblematic of a nation grappling with questions of identity, values, and direction. Yet, even amid deep divisions, there is hope for bridging this divide through dialogue, empathy, and a commitment to shared goals. By fostering a society that values ideological diversity and respects individual expression, America can navigate its challenges while honoring the principles of democracy.

Building a future that embraces both unity and pluralism is not easy, but it is achievable. As Americans engage in dialogue, find common ground, and commit to the strength of a diverse society, they can chart a course forward that reflects the best of both America First and woke ideals. Through mutual respect, constructive engagement, and a spirit of understanding, the nation can transcend its divides and forge a path that honors the contributions and aspirations of all its people.

Final Thoughts on What This Cultural Conflict Reveals About the Evolving American Identity and the Nation's Future

The cultural conflict between the America First and woke movements has exposed profound shifts in American identity, reflecting a nation that is not only evolving but also grappling with what it means to be American in an era defined by rapid change and global interconnection. The clash between these ideologies is more than a political or cultural disagreement; it is an expression of diverging visions for the future of the United States, with each movement representing a different interpretation of American values, priorities, and aspirations.

As we close this exploration of the Trump revolt, America First, and woke politics, it is worth reflecting on what this conflict reveals about the American spirit, and how it might shape the nation's trajectory in the years to come. This ideological struggle highlights key facets of the American identity, including its resilience, diversity, and capacity for reinvention. While these movements have deepened divides, they have also opened up opportunities for reflection, dialogue, and transformation, suggesting that the future of America will be defined by its ability to adapt, evolve, and unify despite these divisions.

A Reflection of Core American Values: Freedom, Equality, and Identity

At the heart of this conflict are three deeply American values: freedom, equality, and identity. Both America First and woke movements are motivated by a desire to uphold these values, even though they interpret them differently. America First advocates emphasize freedom as the right to self-determination, focusing on individual liberty, national sovereignty, and traditional cultural values. In contrast, woke politics frames freedom in terms of liberation from systemic inequalities, advocating for expanded rights and protections to create a more inclusive society.

This ideological tug-of-war underscores America's ongoing struggle to balance freedom with equality, as both sides wrestle with how best to uphold these values in an increasingly diverse nation. The conflict highlights that American identity is not static; it is shaped by the tensions and negotiations between competing visions of what America should stand for. The resilience of these values, and the fervor with which they are defended, demonstrates that despite its divisions, the American spirit remains rooted in a commitment to principles that define the nation, even if their interpretations vary.

The Role of Diversity and Pluralism in American Identity

This cultural clash also highlights the complexities of diversity and pluralism in America. The United States has long been celebrated as a melting pot, a nation where individuals from diverse backgrounds can coexist while pursuing shared dreams. However, the rising tensions between America First and woke ideologies reveal that pluralism is challenging to maintain when core beliefs clash so fundamentally. This divide illustrates that diversity extends beyond ethnicity and race; it encompasses ideological diversity as well, testing America's ability to coexist despite deep-seated differences in values and worldview.

The current ideological divide underscores the importance of building a society that can tolerate, respect, and engage with differing perspectives. As America moves forward, it must grapple with the question of how to honor both ideological diversity and unity. This is a critical juncture in the evolution of American identity, and the nation's ability to embrace pluralism without sacrificing its cohesion will be a testament to its adaptability and resilience.

The American Capacity for Reinvention and Adaptation

The cultural conflict between America First and woke politics also reveals America's remarkable capacity for reinvention and adaptation. Throughout history, the United States has faced periods of intense ideological conflict, from the Civil Rights Movement to debates over immigration and economic policy. Each of these moments forced the nation to confront difficult questions, leading to transformative changes in law, culture, and public policy. The current divide between America First and woke politics may represent another such turning point, as Americans rethink long-standing assumptions and explore new approaches to governance, social justice, and national identity.

The future of American identity may lie in finding a way to integrate aspects of both ideologies, creating a society that honors individual freedoms while promoting inclusivity and justice. This process of adaptation will require open-mindedness, dialogue, and a willingness to innovate. It also calls for an embrace of ambiguity, as Americans learn to accept that the nation's identity is inherently multifaceted, shaped by diverse experiences and evolving values.

Lessons for the Nation's Future: Unity Through Diversity

One of the most significant lessons of this cultural conflict is that unity does not require uniformity. The divisions exposed by the Trump revolt and the rise of woke politics have made it clear that Americans hold diverse, and often contradictory, views about their country's values, future, and role in the world. The challenge for America is to foster a sense of unity that respects these differences, embracing diversity as a source of strength rather than division.

Achieving this unity through diversity will require cultivating a culture that values empathy, mutual respect, and collaboration. America's future success depends on its ability to create an environment where differing perspectives can coexist constructively, contributing to a shared sense of purpose. The process of bridging these divides will not be easy, but it is essential for building a society that reflects the ideals of democracy, freedom, and justice. If America can rise to this challenge, it will emerge stronger, more inclusive, and better equipped to lead in an increasingly complex world.

Conclusion: The Unfinished American Experiment

The Trump revolt and the ideological divide between America First and woke politics are reminders that America's identity is an ongoing experiment, one that requires constant reflection, dialogue, and growth. As a nation built on ideals rather than a single ethnic or cultural identity, the United States has always had to navigate competing visions for its future. This current cultural conflict is the latest chapter in that story, reflecting a society wrestling with how to adapt to new realities while honoring its foundational values.

While the future of American identity remains uncertain, this conflict has revealed both the challenges and the possibilities inherent in the American experiment. The path forward will depend on the nation's ability to learn from this moment, to recognize that diversity and unity are not mutually exclusive, and to commit to the values that bind Americans together even in times of division. By engaging with these questions openly and honestly, America has the potential not only to bridge its divides but also to redefine itself for a new era, building a future that honors its past while embracing the transformative power of change.

In the end, the ideological conflict between America First and woke politics is a testament to the vibrancy and complexity of American society. It underscores that America is not defined by one set of beliefs or values but by a tapestry of perspectives woven together by a shared commitment to democracy, freedom, and progress. As the nation moves forward, this commitment will be its greatest asset, guiding it through the challenges and opportunities of the 21st century as it continues to evolve, adapt, and pursue the vision of a more perfect union.

References

Books on Populism, Nationalism, and Political Movements

Mudde, Cas, and Cristóbal Rovira Kaltwasser. Populism: A Very Short Introduction. Oxford University Press, 2017.

This book provides a concise overview of populism as a political phenomenon, useful for contextualizing the rise of Trump's America First movement within broader populist trends.

Fukuyama, Francis. Identity: The Demand for Dignity and the Politics of Resentment. Farrar, Straus and Giroux, 2018.

Fukuyama's exploration of identity politics offers insights into the forces that drive both America First and woke ideologies, especially in the context of political polarization.

Hochschild, Arlie Russell. Strangers in Their Own Land: Anger and Mourning on the American Right. The New Press, 2016.

This book examines the emotional and cultural underpinnings of the American right, providing context for the rise of Trump's movement and his supporters' motivations.

Glaeser, Edward, and Andrei Shleifer. A Nation of Gamblers: Real Estate Speculation and American Inequality. Harvard University Press, 2014.

Glaeser's exploration of inequality helps frame economic concerns that play into both populist America First and progressive woke ideologies.

Judis, John B. The Populist Explosion: How the Great Recession Transformed American and European Politics. Columbia Global Reports, 2016.

This book discusses the rise of populism across the West, shedding light on the cultural and economic drivers behind Trump's appeal.

Books on Trump, America First Policies, and Nationalism

Trump, Donald J. Crippled America: How to Make America Great Again. Threshold Editions, 2015.

Trump's own words provide insight into the America First philosophy and the policies that defined his presidency.

Sullivan, Sean. America First: Understanding the Trump Doctrine. CreateSpace Independent Publishing Platform, 2018.

This analysis focuses on the America First doctrine as a cohesive policy and examines its implications on foreign policy, trade, and nationalism.

Luce, Edward. The Retreat of Western Liberalism. Atlantic Monthly Press, 2017.

Luce's analysis of Western political shifts contextualizes the cultural and ideological environment that gave rise to Trump's America First movement.

Haidt, Jonathan. The Righteous Mind: Why Good People Are Divided by Politics and Religion. Vintage, 2012.

Haidt's insights on moral psychology provide a valuable framework for understanding the division between America First and woke perspectives.

Rauch, Jonathan. The Constitution of Knowledge: A Defense of Truth. Brookings Institution Press, 2021.

Rauch's defense of truth-seeking institutions is relevant for discussions on fake news, media polarization, and the cultural divide in America.

Books on Woke Politics, Social Justice, and Progressive Movements

DiAngelo, Robin. White Fragility: Why It's So Hard for White People to Talk About Racism. Beacon Press, 2018.

DiAngelo's book provides a perspective on woke culture's emphasis on racial justice and is frequently referenced in discussions of social justice activism.

Kendi, Ibram X. How to Be an Antiracist. One World, 2019.

Kendi's work is central to understanding the woke movement's focus on structural racism and social justice.

Bok, Derek. The Politics of Happiness: What Government Can Learn from the New Research on Well-Being. Princeton University Press, 2010.

Bok explores well-being and its intersections with social justice, adding depth to the understanding of progressive policy motivations.

Abrams, Stacey. Our Time is Now: Power, Purpose, and the Fight for a Fair America. Henry Holt and Co., 2020.

Abrams' insights into voting rights and equity efforts reflect the values and goals of woke politics, providing context for its influence on American identity.

West, Cornel. Race Matters. Beacon Press, 1993.

Though older, West's work remains foundational for understanding the philosophical roots of woke politics and its impact on American social thought.

Scholarly Articles and Journals

Inglehart, Ronald, and Pippa Norris. "Trump, Brexit, and the Rise of Populism: Economic Have-Nots and Cultural Backlash." Harvard Kennedy School Working Paper No. RWP16-026, 2016.

This paper explores economic and cultural factors contributing to the rise of populism, relevant for understanding the foundation of America First and woke politics.

Wells, Christopher, et al. "Trump, Brexit, and the Media: Examining Public Opinion in the Context of Online News Consumption." Journal of Communication, vol. 68, no. 3, 2018, pp. 420-441.

Examines the role of media in shaping public opinion on populist movements, contributing to the analysis of media's role in America First and woke debates.

Kreiss, Daniel, and Shannon C. McGregor. "Technology Firms Shape Political Communication: The Work of Microsoft, Facebook, Twitter, and Google with Campaigns during the 2016 U.S. Presidential Cycle." Political Communication, vol. 35, no. 2, 2018, pp. 155-177.

This article highlights the influence of technology firms on political communication, relevant to discussions of social media's role in ideological divides.

Mutz, Diana C. "Status Threat, Not Economic Hardship, Explains the 2016 Presidential Vote." Proceedings of the National Academy of Sciences, vol. 115, no. 19, 2018, pp. E4330-E4339.

Mutz's research on the role of status threat in Trump's election offers insights into the cultural roots of America First support.

Zimdars, Melissa, and Kembrew McLeod, eds. Fake News: Understanding Media and Misinformation in the Digital Age. MIT Press, 2020.

This edited collection provides an in-depth look at misinformation in the digital age, relevant for understanding the cultural polarization between America First and woke politics.

News Outlets and Media Reports

Pew Research Center. "Political Polarization in the American Public." Pew Research Center, 2017.

Provides data on polarization trends in America, helping contextualize the cultural divide.

The Atlantic, New York Times, Washington Post, Fox News, Breitbart News.

Articles and op-eds from these news sources offer perspectives from both sides of the ideological spectrum, reflecting the broader media landscape that influences public opinion.

Government and Policy Reports

U.S. Census Bureau. "Income and Poverty in the United States: 2020."

Provides data on income inequality, relevant to discussions of economic concerns shared by both America First and woke advocates.

Congressional Research Service. "Trade Policy: An Overview." CRS Report R45148, updated 2021.

Analyzes U.S. trade policies, offering context for America First economic perspectives.

Author Name: James T. Wallace

Biography:

James T. Wallace is an independent political analyst, historian, and author known for his in-depth explorations of contemporary cultural and ideological movements in America. With a background in sociology and political science from Georgetown University, Wallace has spent over two decades analyzing the shifting dynamics of American identity, national policy, and grassroots movements. His writing reflects a balanced approach, examining both the historical roots and current manifestations of ideological divides in the United States.

A former journalist and editor for several policy journals, Wallace has covered the rise of populist movements, the impact of globalization on rural communities, and the cultural forces behind the so-called "woke" revolution. His deep understanding of the socio-political landscape allows him to delve into complex topics with clarity, shedding light on the motivations and concerns that drive both sides of the political spectrum. In The Trump Revolt: Putting America First in a Woke World, Wallace combines his passion for research with a nuanced perspective, aiming to foster dialogue and understanding amid America's growing ideological divide.

Wallace lives in Charlottesville, Virginia, where he continues to write and consult on political and cultural issues. When he's not working on his latest project, he can be found hiking the Blue Ridge Mountains or engaging in spirited debates with his community on the future of American democracy.

Disclaimer:

This book, The Trump Revolt: Putting America First in a Woke World, is intended for informational and educational purposes only. The views and opinions expressed in this book reflect the author's interpretations of current cultural and ideological trends in America and are not meant to endorse, criticize, or disparage any political group, party, or individual.

While every effort has been made to ensure the accuracy and reliability of the information presented, readers are encouraged to conduct their own research and consult a variety of sources to form a well-rounded perspective. This book does not represent legal, financial, or political advice and should not be treated as such.

The author and publisher do not assume any responsibility for actions taken by readers based on the content of this book. Any references to individuals, organizations, or specific events are used solely to provide context and should not be interpreted as endorsements or affiliations. The inclusion of certain perspectives is meant to foster understanding and dialogue and does not imply that the author or publisher advocates for or against any particular ideology.

Copyright and Legal Notice